EGYPT
THE
PRAETORIAN
STATE

EGYPT THE PRAETORIAN STATE

AMOS PERLMUTTER

Transaction Books
New Brunswick, New Jersey

Library of Congress Catalog Number: 73-85100
ISBN: 0-87855-085-2

Printed in the United States of America.

CONTENTS

PREFACE

Every book has a history. This one's history is interesting only because it evolved in a period, the 1960s, when the political science profession was in search of new intellectual vistas. Unfortunately, only one flower ever bloomed—the comparative-theoretical school. At the time, some of the leading members of the profession and, especially, younger scholars perceived that political science, as a profession, was lagging behind the more "advanced" fields of anthropology, sociology and social psychology. "Advanced" meant "scientific"—rigorous and formal approaches. Concommitantly, the Committee of Comparative Politics of the Social Science Research Council decreed that research in comparative politics should encompass the emerging ex-colonial states. In the end, however, it concentrated solely on "developing politics." A universal comparative theory was formulated that was designed to analyze and explain events in Gabon, the central African Republic and Western Europe, in all times and in all places. This *Gleichschaltung* orientation sent students and established scholars on safaris into other fields. Anthropology and sociology of the Malinowski, Evans-Pritchard, and Parsonian vintage became fashionable, to mention only a few of the newly discovered professional saints of comparative politics. From the middle 1950s to the early 1960s, a new type of comparative politics proliferated, whose paradigm (to paraphrase Kuhn) and whose science was etched in a textbook by Gabriel Almond and James Coleman, *The Politics of Developing Areas* (1960). This was followed by a seven volume series by the same Committee of Comparative Politics, published by Princeton University Press between 1963-1973.

Those of us who were not inspired by the pseudo-science of this new school of comparative politics worked alone, deprived of the rewards bestowed on and by the corporate professionals of political science. Funds for research, professional mobility and recognition were selectively distributed. Going unrewarded did not matter so much; what stung was being labeled "traditionalist." For the traditionalists will not be satisfied with this study either.

In the study of the modern Middle East historiographers, scribologists and linguistic orientations, nineteenth-century style, still dominate. Islamists, Arabists, cultural historians and traditional anthropologists are still unwilling to make use of the benefits of modern theories on power, authority and political structures, confining themselves to interpretation of documents and the usual methods of cultural history. This study is a pioneer effort to analyze and interpret political power in Egypt, using "praetorianism," a concept of political power and a typology of political structures and of new institutions in Egypt. It is neither inspired by the rigid universalism of the comparative-theoretical political science school, nor by factologists of the old world academies whose roots date back to the turn of the century. The completion of this study took much longer than it might have required in a more tolerable intellectual atmosphere. A decade is too long for any author to spend on a study of this kind. Mea culpa.

ACKNOWLEDGMENTS

Every book has many handmaidens. This one should not have had so many. Yet for the reasons mentioned in the preface, I doubt if this book would have seen the light of day without the support of many dedicated friends and loyal colleagues. While they cannot be held responsible for the worth of my efforts, I owe them my heartfelt thanks for standing by me at all times.

First and foremost, I am grateful to Nina Perlmutter, without whom I might not have believed that the book was worth the effort. I am grateful to another woman, who prefers anonymity, for urging me to publish the book and to do it soon. I thank Charles Hutchinson of the Air Force Office of Scientific Research for granting me unlimited resources and for years of friendship and confidence. Samuel P. Huntington of Harvard is a man of deep conviction: I am grateful to him for standing with me against unfriendly and unfair critics, for unfailing efforts toward the publication of this book, and for giving me the unique opportunity to join the Center for International Affairs at Harvard.

Seymour Martin Lipset, a founding father of a contemporary school of American political sociology, supported me at Berkeley and at Harvard and opened the academic gates for my ideas at the time when my style of political science was not fashionable. My late friend and colleague Joseph Levenson of Berkeley, a warm person and a scholar in the Spinozian tradition and with Proustian vision, died too soon to see this book, whose subtitle was his idea. Franz Schurmann, Daniel Lev, Liisa North, Clement Moore, Zeev Brenner and Ariel Bloch, all of Berkeley, gave me advice, helped me formulate my ideas and led me to modify certain aspects of the style and approach of this book.

My friends in Israel in the great centers of Middle Eastern Studies at Tel-Aviv and Jerusalem were a great help, especially Moshe Ma'oz, Shimon Shamir, Meir Pa'il and especially Sarah Lulko. Every student of the Arab military owes a debt to Eliezer Be'eri's work on the military in the Middle East. Be'eri was also generous enough to read parts of manuscript and to kindly but fiercely disagree. Elie Kedourie of the London School of Economics, a historian in the classical tradition, influenced my ideas and offered his friendship even when he disagreed. Moshe Lissak of the Hebrew University was a constant companion; I learned much from his extensive experience with the role of the military in politics in underdeveloped countries. Maury Feld of Harvard sharpened my mind no end in countless conversations. Although I never studied with Gabriel Baer or Elie Kedourie, their impact on this study is manifest. Baer's and Kedourie's works have convinced me that the great tradition of Oriental scholars can be maintained and is fruitful—even though my approach will cause them no end of agony. No student of the Modern Middle East can maintain his reputation without being an avid reader of *Hamizrah Hehadash (The New East)* published by the Israel Oriental Society. This is a solid and unfailing source of information and ideas and if it did not inspire the style of this book, at least it shaped my convictions.

The encyclopedic *Middle East Record* published by the Shiloah Middle Eastern Institute of the University of Tel-Aviv has been a constant companion as well as Menahem Mansoor's voluminous *Arab World,* a major political and diplomatic reference book on the Middle East. Last but not least I owe a debt to Itzchak Oron, whose impact on this book is felt everywhere. I am most grateful to the Center for International Affairs at Harvard, its director, my colleagues and the secretaries for all they did for me. Benjamin Read, former Director of the Woodrow Wilson Center for International Scholars and members of the center during the year 1971-72, especially Frances Hunter, gave me a wonderful year of free time and intellectual stimulation in Washington, where I was able to complete this work. I am grateful to my publisher, Irving Louis Horowitz, for years of dialectical relationship, to Abdul Aziz Said of American University, a real friend, and to Mary E. Curtis, my editor.

GLOSSARY

AL-ISTI'MAR

Imperialism. In Arabic the literal meaning is "to civilize"; it also means "the devil."

ARAB SOCIALIST UNION (ASU)

Nasser's third attempt to form a Nasserite dominated party, charted on June 30, 1962; it has changed forms several times since, and is now almost defunct.

BA'TH

Ba'th means "Renaissance." Begun as a coterie of teachers and politicians in Beirut, Lebanon between 1947-1949, it later moved to Damascus. It was united with the Hawrani Socialist party in 1953, then became the Ba'th Arab Socialist Party. Since 1958 it has become international and has branched into several Arab countries. Now (1973), dominated by the military in the regimes of both Syria and Iraq.

CALIPH (Khalifa)

"Successor" (i.e., of Muhammed), a title assumed by temporal and spiritual rulers in Muhammedan countries. Since Muhammed was the seal of the Prophets, Abu Bakr the successor (Khalifa), founded the caliphate, an institution which lasted for centuries.

CIRCASSIANS

Also known as CERKS, from the northwest, i.e. Ibero-Caucasian. They settled on the Sea of Azov and the Black Sea.

CONSTITUTIONALISTS

A group formed by modernist students sent to Europe for technical training. From the group emerged, among others, a coterie of politicians formed around a newspaper *Al-Mu'ayyad*. In 1907 they formed the People's party and the Nationalist (Watani) party.

COPT

An Egyptian of the native race descended from the ancient Egyptians, especially a member of the Coptic church, the ancient Christian church of Egypt, now surviving mainly among fellahin.

FEDDAN

1.038 acres of land.

FELLAH (pl. fellahin)

A peasant or agricultural laborer in Egypt, Syria, or other Arabic-speaking country. One of a race type in modern Egypt descended from ancient Egyptians.

FOC

Free Officers Corps. The clandestine army cabal organized by Nassar in 1949, in existence until 1952.

FREE OFFICERS

A differentiated and undefined group of officers within the Egyptian army who plotted to overthrow the monarchy between 1938-1952.

IKHTARNA LAK

"We Have Chosen For You" series. A series of publications of the Liberation Institute to create a Nasserite ideology, published between 1953-1957.

JANISSARY

A soldier of a body of Turkish infantry that existed from the fourteenth century. First, they were slaves; eventually they became the main fighting force of the Turks, until abolished in 1826. Also, any Turkish soldier.

KHEDIVE

The ruler of Egypt, 1867-1914, governing as a semi-independent viceroy of the sultan of Turkey.

MAMELUKE

One of a body of soldiers recruited from slaves converted to Islam, who had great political power in Egypt (the Mameluke Sultans, 1250-1517) until exterminated or dispersed by Muhammed 'Ali in 1811. A fighting slave, in Muhammedan countries.

MISR AL-FATAT PARTY

Young Egypt. Founded by a lawyer, Ahmad Husayn, as an association of students in 1933. In 1938 became a political party. Inspired both Nasser and Sadat.

MBs

Members of the Muslim Brotherhood.

MUSLIM BROTHERHOOD

A fundamentalist neo-Islamic movement first organized by Sheikh Hasan al-Banna in Isma'lia, the Suez Canal, in 1928, organizing among Egypt's modernizing but politically frustrated middle classes. Egypt's only mass movement. Estimated at over 3 million members in 1947. Played a key role in the initiation of Nasserism.

MURSHID

Spiritual head and fighter for the faith.

MUHAMMAD 'ALI

The modernizer of Egypt; wanted to establish dynastic rule (1805-1848) and take over the caliphate and the Ottoman Empire.

MUSLIM LEAGUE

A secularist Pakistani organization.

NEUER MITTELSTAND

New middle class. Coined by professors Lederer and Marschak in 1926 referring to the salaried classes.

PASHA

Formerly, an honorary title, placed after the name, given to officers of high rank in Turkey.

QA'IDAH SHA'BIYYAH

The Popular Base; an elective body at the bottom of the National Union pyramid, established in 1958.

RAIS

Political and moral leader.

REVOLUTIONARY COMMAND COUNCIL (RCC)

The executive committee of the Liberation Rally, between 1953-1955.

SHAYKHS

The heads of the guilds, same as sheikhs.

SHEIKH

An Arab tribal chief.

SUFISM

Tendency in religion toward fundamentalist puritanism.

SULTAN

A ruler of a Muhammedan state; a title of any Muhammedan prince. Specifically, the ruler of the Turks.

AL-TALI'AH

A magazine, representing ASU left-wing views, active from 1967-1970; now defunct.

TA'IFAH

Guild or corporation; the characteristic feature of a town's social organization, and the core of medieval Islamic culture.

THE TRIPLE REVOLUTION OF EGYPT

National, Arab and social.

ULEMA

A body of scholars trained in Moslem religion and law.

'UMDAH

Village notables in Egypt.

WAFD PARTY

Al-Wafd al-Misri. The Egyptian Delegation. Egypt's first movement for independence, named after the delegation formed by Sa'd Zaghlul and a few others representing Egypt before the Peace Conference of 1919. Wafd was officially proclaimed in November 1918. Eventually declined into a party of absentee landlords and rural aristocrats. Abolished by Nasser in 1954.

INTRODUCTION

The Nasserite regime has been the subject of many studies. Some have used primary source material in Arabic, others, material that exists in translation. But the clandestine nature of the Free Officers and the personalized character of Nasserist rule have always precluded intimate, direct, reliable and extensive information about this regime and especially about the Officer Corps. With the exception of the Lacourtures' description of the rise of the Free Officers in *Egypt in Transition*[1] (Capricorn, New York, 1962), few authors can claim intimate contact with sources or individuals in Nasser's Egypt.

Manfred Halpern, for instance, admits that "we know little about the internal structure of the military bureaucracy in the Middle East,"[2] and Leonard Binder concedes

1

that "we must own to the fact that we have at present little solid information about the social composition of the Egyptian officer corps."[3] While Morroe Berger has provided valuable information concerning civil servants in the Ministries of Education and Agriculture, the crucial ministries—defense, the armed services—and the Arab Socialist executives have not received equal treatment, simply because adequate information has not been available, and the latter did not exist when Berger wrote his book. In view of the fragmentary nature of the material available, it has been possible to determine only approximate viewpoints and make only tentative estimates about the Nasserite regime. Since the present writer does not claim to have more information at his disposal than other scholars, this study is limited to the analysis and interpretation of a few significant aspects of Nasser's Egypt. My purpose is primarily to define the patterns of political behavior existing in Egypt today, and to direct attention, especially for future students of Egypt, away from what has been the primary object of other students of Nasser's Egypt—either an apologetic or a futile, psuedo-social science effort to explain away the Nasser dictatorship in favor of a progressive regime model.

This volume challenges several of the premature interpretations current in the social sciences, such as the "new middle class" theory, the theory of the "integrative revolution" and others, as well as the rather extravagant expectation of some social scientists dealing with the Nasserite phenomenon, that he was Egypt's only hope, best ruler and a model for all other Afro-Asian peoples. *Egypt: The Praetorian State* deals with Nasser's failure to establish sustaining and viable political institutions and structures, the failure of his ideology at the organizational level, and his successful development of a personalist and praetorian rule—the only type of rule, in fact, that Nasser ever successfully pursued. There is particular emphasis on the unique role Nasser assigned to the army, and the subsequent failure of that body to further any purpose other than Nasser's and its own.

In many ways the strategy of Nasserite rule is reminiscent of that employed by Egypt's first great modernizer, Muhammed 'Ali—sultanist-patrimonial rule based on dependent manipulation and control. Like Muhammed 'Ali, Nasser was an empire-builder, but he built a nation instead of an empire.[4] Nasser differed from Muhammed 'Ali primarily in his responsiveness to the cultural, social and ideological demands of the modernizing-nationalist revolution.

The survival of a Nasserite type regime after Nasser will probably continue to depend on the amount of support the praetorian ruler receives from a small number of politically isolated elites, particularly the armed forces. The stability of Sadat's regime, will depend on his ability to manipulate a few military-intelligence and bureaucratic elites. For Egypt has made little progress since 1952 in the formation of reasonably autonomous or sustaining political institutions and structures. Personal rule and the particular strategies invented by Muhammed 'Ali and carried on by his successors are still the crucial instruments for maintaining praetorian regimes in Egypt.

1. MILITARY PRAETORIANISM: A NEW TYPE OF POLITICS

Praetorianism

Egypt is a praetorian state: a state in which the military has the potential of dominating the political system. Its political processes favor the development of the army as the core group and as a political ruling class, since Egypt's political leadership (as distinguished from its bureaucratic, administrative and managerial leadership) is primarily recruited from the army.

In a praetorian state the military plays a highly significant role in key political structures and institutions. In Egypt, the military effects and sustains constitutional changes which, in a nonpraetorian state, would be executed by other institutions. In a praetorian state the army intervenes in the government frequently; whereas, in a nonpraetorian state, it does so only rarely.

4

Praetorian government develops when civilian institutions lack legitimacy. In the nonpraetorian state, the citizen conforms to the government's laws even when he considers them detrimental to his personal interests, because he accepts the legitimacy of the law.[1] A nonpraetorian state is governed with the consent of the people[2] but, in a praetorian state, the people hold their consent in abeyance because they believe the proscriptions of the family, the clan, the tribe or the church hold precedence over the laws of the state. Thus, individuals in a praetorian state tend to disobey laws detrimental to their personal interests, and to question governmental action if it does not respond to their demands.

Praetorianism has existed in all historical periods. In view of recent events in underdeveloped countries, it may even be said that praetorianism represents a normal stage within any nation's development. At present, praetorianism often appears in states which are in the early stages of modernization and industrialization.[3] In underdeveloped nations, the army is propelled into political action because civilian groups have failed to legitimize themselves; thus, the army's presence in civilian affairs indicates the civilian government's inability to control internal corruption.[4] The lack of both material improvements and ideological perspectives often correlates with the development of praetorianism in underdeveloped countries.[5] Traditional institutions are unable to cope with the changes brought by material improvement; and, at the same time, the modern institutions which are needed to direct such changes are difficult to organize because of the traditional orientation of the people. In the ensuing disorganization, both the country's economic and ideological development suffer setbacks.

Conditions conducive to praetorianism may exist in a state in which the army has not yet demonstrated its power to intervene in politics. However, when these conditions are accompanied by other supporting conditions, the chances for army intervention increase.

This study attempts to identify the historical, socioeconomic and political conditions which contributed to the rise and persistence of praetorianism in Egypt. It briefly characterizes the praetorian army and describes the two praetorian army types—arbitrator and ruler—as they have developed in Egypt.

Through the examination of concrete historical situations, both the characteristics and the nature of the praetorian state are identified. These are then analyzed in terms of Weberian ideal types, which are especially useful in distinguishing arbitration from ruler type armies and praetorianism in general from military praetorianism. What is introduced here is a Weberian ideal type construct which does not necessarily exhaust empirical reality but which attempts to isolate, accentuate and articulate elements of a recurrent political phenomenon—the praetorian army and the praetorian state.

In general, the conditions contributing to underdevelopment also contribute to praetorianism, since they represent general structural and political weaknesses (See Table 1). What distinguishes a praetorian state from a nonpraetorian, underdeveloped state is the former's dependence on military rule. Praetorianism, and particularly military praetorianism, can be explained by a multitude of preconditions including: a rapid mobilization of men, groups and resources; a low degree of social cohesion; high social polarity; a low level of political institutionalization; an asymmetrical relationship between urban center and periphery; and ineffective support for sustained political structures and procedures.

Military praetorianism is a special case of praetorianism. We distinguish military praetorianism from general prae-

Table 1: CORRELATES OF PRAETORIANISM

CORRELATES	Praetorian State	Nonpraetorian State
General:		
Potential for state to be dominated by the military	High	Low
Development of the military as core group and ruling class	High	Low
Government recruits political leaders from the military	Frequently	Infrequently
Potential for military intervention	High	Low
Social:		
Degree of social cohesion	Low	High
Social polarity	High	Low
Social efforts to mobilize population	Unsuccessful	Successful
Political:		
Level of political institutionalization	Low	High
Support for political structures	Sporadic	Sustained
Efforts of political parties	Ineffective	Effective
Frequency of civilian intervention in the army	High	Low
Military:		
Cohesiveness	Low	High
Receptiveness to foreign intervention	High	Low
Tradition of professionalism	Not Established	Established
Praetorian tradition	Long	Short

torianism on the basis of the interaction between the
military organization and the praetorian state. In all
praetorian states, the military is oriented toward political
intervention. But it could rule in alliance with civilians or
temporarily act as an arbitrator of civilian power. A
military praetorian state exists only when the ruler-prae-
torian, or its modified version, prevails or is predominant.

Two Types of Praetorian Armies

The two basic types of praetorian armies are the
arbitrator type and the ruler type. The former tends to be
more professional oriented, with no independent political
organization and little interest in manufacturing a political
ideology. The latter has an independent political organization and, in some cases, a fairly coherent and elaborate
political ideology.

The arbitrator type army imposes a time limit on its
own rule and arranges to hand over the government to an
"acceptable" civilian regime. However, the arbitrator type
army does not necessarily relinquish its political influence
when it returns to the barracks; in fact, in many cases it
continues to act as a trustee and guardian of civilian
authority and political stability. Such, for instance, is the
essence of the Kemalist legacy in Turkey; there the army
serves as the permanent guardian of the Constitution.[6] If
the conditions for the return of a civilian regime are not
fulfilled, an arbitrator army may eventually become a ruler
army. (The Syrian military is a shining example of the
latter. This has also become true in Latin American
praetorian states since the 1900s.) The ruler army is not
committed to a time limit on its own rule; nor does it
make any provision for its eventual return to the barracks.

The arbitrator type of praetorian army tends to preserve military professionalism. By professionalism we mean professional training, the emulation of skill and the preservation of professional collective integrity—i.e. corporatism.* It is conservative, and generally tends to maximize civilian power.[8] The ruler type army, although it does not abandon professionalism, subordinates it to political considerations. In general, the ruler type army prefers to maximize military rule, with a view toward establishing direct and permanent military control.

Both types of praetorian armies are politically committed; the difference between them lies in their attitudes toward their political roles. Since the ruler army has an independent political organization, it creates ideology to legitimize its rule. If an army does not produce an ideology, it must identify with a progressive and popular ideology created elsewhere.

Although the arbitrator army tends to be more conservative and the ruler army more radical, we find ideologically motivated radicals and conservatives in both types. However, ideological orientation is not the real demarcation line between the two types of praetorianism. The chief difference between them is their orientation toward intervention and direct military rule. On the whole praetorian armies do not generate political ideologies. However, they are influenced, if not when they actually rule, then in the barracks, by political modes—or, more directly, by civilian ideologies or politicians. Thus, the two types of armies can be placed on a left-right continuum.

---

*Samuel P. Huntington, in *The Soldier and the State,*[7] defines military professionalism as the military's objective attitude to politics that is, nonintervention. He also puts a very high premium on the military's role as the instrument of the state. For a full analysis of the concept of military professionalism see Amos Perlmutter, *Military and Politics in Modern Times,* forthcoming (part 1).

The actions of both types are conditioned by: the internal structure of the army and the extent to which it has developed an identifiable political organization; the army's interaction with civilian organizations; and the type of political order the army desires to eliminate and the type of replacement it has in mind.

Military praetorianism may also arise from special conditions within the military establishment itself, such as frequent military coups, countercoups and interventions, fratricide within the Officer Corps, a lack of military professional tradition and, of course, the long reign of the praetorian tradition, all of which have some political

Table 2: ATTITUDES AND BEHAVIOR OF THE TWO TYPES OF PRAETORIAN ARMIES

ATTITUDE OR BEHAVIOR	Arbitrator type army	Ruler type army
Attitude toward existing social order before the army intervened	Acceptance	Rejection
Attitude toward return to the barracks after civilian disputes are settled	Positive	Negative
Attitude toward political organization of the army	Rejection	Acceptance
Length of time that army plans to stay in power	Until an "acceptable" alternative regime is established	No time limit
Attitude toward military professionalism	Positive	Negative
Method of political operation	Covert	Overt
Attitude toward civilian retribution against military intervention	Fear	No fear

importance. But simply identifying these variables is not enough; we must also explain the connections among them. How and when do they lead to military praetorianism? Why is the "praetorian society" only subject to the potential domination of the military, rather than, for example, that of the students, the unions, the clergy or other professional politicized elites? Samuel P. Huntington has established that no single explanation can account for the phenomenon of military praetorianism. "Military explanations do not explain military interventions. The reason for this is simply that military interventions are only one specific manifestation of a broader phenomenon in underdeveloped societies: the general politicization of social forces and institutions."[9]

Political Conditions Contributing to Praetorianism

Low level of political institutionalization and lack of sustained support for political structures. According to Huntington, "the strength of political organizations and procedures varies with their *scope of support* and their *level of institutionalization.*"[10] In praetorian states the level of support of political organizations, that is, the number and diversity of citizens belonging to such organizations, is low. Thus, political parties tend to be fragmented; each one is supported by separate, unrelated social groups. The labor movement is similarly fragmented: each category of worker has a separate union, and the unions distrust one another. These phenomena are political manifestations of the lack of social cohesion common to praetorian states.

The level of institutionalization—the degree to which political organizations develop their own traditions and

become able to act autonomously—is also low in praetorian states. Although the traditional political institutions, incapable of dealing with recent social and economic
changes, have been eliminated, the newly-established, more
flexible institutions have not yet been widely accepted.
Their general acceptance is often hampered by the degree
to which they represent particular small interest groups.
Huntington also notes the frequency of military intervention in states where institutionalization has not taken
place.[11]

A state may exhibit most of the social characteristics of
praetorianism, while its political institutions and procedures remain relatively stable. In such a case, the state's
political institutions will be able to act fairly freely, and
army intervention will be rare. Such a state is not
praetorian, but it may become so. (India is a non-prae-
torian nation which fits this description.) It must be
emphasized that the presence of some praetorian conditions does not necessarily lead to army intervention.
Conversely, army intervention may occur even though
some praetorian conditions are missing.

Weak and ineffective political parties. Weak and ineffective political parties, another condition that encourages
praetorianism, are manifestations of a low level of political
institutionalization. Strong parties, conversely, have been
the most successful agents of political institutionalization,
which in turn helps to eliminate conditions that lead to
praetorianism.

Few underdeveloped countries have strong political
parties of the pluralistic type. In Egypt, the *Wafd* party
was taken over by landowning interests and thus lost the
support of other politically articulate and new forces.
When a political party represents particular interests in this
way, its leaders become less effective in promoting projects

necessary for the economic growth and integration of their country as a whole. The decline of the Egyptian party system and Nasser's futile efforts to replace it with the Arab Socialist Union party will be examined at length later in this volume. The absence of a strong political party system in Egypt is a direct result of Nasser's military praetorianism.

Frequent civilian intervention in the military. Military intervention in civilian affairs is usually not precipitated by the military groups themselves. In general, civilians turn to the military for political support when civilian political structures and institutions fail, factionalism develops, and constitutional means for the conduct of political action are unavailable. Thereafter, the civilians begin to indoctrinate the military with their own political ideologies. Several examples of this process can be found in the Middle East and in Latin America.

In Turkey the Committee for Union and Progress, founded by the Young Turks, brought about the 1908 revolution which brought the Young Turk movement to power. More recently, the People's Party, or at least its affiliates among the officers, intervened indirectly in the Turkish coups of 1960-1961. Menderes, then Turkey's minister and head of the Justice Party, frequently interfered in military affairs and meddled with military appointments. In modern Greece, the political parties meddled for so long in the military that, in 1907, the latter turned against the monarchy, the political parties, and individuals who frequently intervened in and thereby politicized the army.

Elsewhere in the Middle East, extremist nationalist politicans began the indoctrination and infiltration of the military. The Iraqi nationalists, led by the nationalist Ahali group, accomplished a series of coups and countercoups in

Iraq between 1936 and 1941, and the army, since that initial participation, has not withdrawn from the political scene. Between 1940 and 1950, the Iraqi army contributed to the establishment and maintenance of a relatively stable government under Nuri al-sa'id.

In Egypt, the Muslim Brotherhood and Young Egypt *(Misr al-Fatat)*, two important nationalist and fascist movements, have collaborated with Egyptian army officers since the late 1930s.[12] The *Ba'th* party and the Arab Socialist Party, led by the latter's founder, the Syrian revolutionary Akram Haurani, transformed the Syrian army from an obscure colonial force into the most militant nationalist force in Syria. Since that time most of the more than 25 successful and unsuccessful coups in Syria have been initiated or sponsored by the new Arab Ba'th Socialist Party, which emerged from the union of the two original parties.

Other factors, such as defeat in war, the death of a powerful army leader, foreign interventions, and conflicts among senior and junior military officers, are typical secondary causes of praetorianism.[13] However, if the primary causes are absent, these secondary causes alone cannot bring about a praetorian state.

The most obvious characteristic of modern military elites in developing polities is their aspiration toward military professionalism and corporatism—that is, control over the military organization. The professionalism and institutionalization of the military entails the establishment of military colleges, specialized training, and the formation of a collective corporate group and a national army.* Praetorian conditions are often related to profes-

---

*By corporatism we again mean the collective effort of a professional group to maintain its integrity, to preserve its autonomy and to regulate the recruitment, promotion and advancement of its membership.

sional military establishments, such as the military acade-my, and structures, such as the corporate officer group, some of which are institutionalized before concomitant political and socioeconomic structures—such as political parties, parliaments, a centralized administrative bureau-cracy, national authority, middle classes and a nationalist ideology—are institutionalized. Thus, corporate profession-alism is not a guarantee against military praetorianism. In fact, in many praetorian states the military interventionists are the corporate professional soldiers, the graduates of the military academies. In theory, at least, political activity is contrary to the standards and professional ethics of the military. But a professional stance does not guarantee the political objectivity of the officer class. Even in praetorian states, the remnants of professionalism may survive, creating conflicts between formally adopted professional norms and the realities of politics. These conflicts, however, tend to draw a widening circle of political activists from the officer corps. This, in turn, encourages the Officer Corps to break into factions and cliques.

An army may display most of the standard characteris-tics of the ruler type army, including a well-articulated ideology to which the Officer Corps adheres, without actually ruling. An example of this situation is the Peruvian army.[14] In such a case, the army presents a unified point of view and stabilizes civilian governments which hold views similar to its own. The army's projects are freely developed, and it may advocate its position openly in journals such as the *Actualidad Militar,* publish-ed by the Peruvian army.[15] On the other hand, in some cases arbitrator armies have ruled for extended periods of time. Examples of this type include the Latin American *caudillismo,* and the Iraqi officers who have ruled Iraq since its independence.

The Ruler Type Praetorian Army

The ruler type of praetorian army has several basic characteristics: First, and most important, typical modern ruler type praetorians represent only a very small segment of the Officer Corps. The politically oriented officers are never more than 20 percent of the total corps; and the politically active officers comprise 5 percent or less.*[16] Therefore, the ruling group is always small, clandestine and conspiratorial. This small number of politically active officers comes to power through a military coup; they then establish a political system which is generally decimated by personal and organizational rivalries. In some cases, however, the ruler type of army is sustained, by becoming a one-man military dictatorship. To reiterate, praetorian rule is not always military rule; but praetorian rule requires the support of a military establishment if it is to persist.

Throughout developing countries, traditional parliamentary politics and liberalism have become identified by the military with status quo politics—colonial, corrupt, not "revolutionary" and inefficient. The ruler type praetorian army increasingly tends to abandon existing institutions, ideologies and procedures in favor of modernization, industrialization and the mobilization of organizational structures as they are proposed in theoretical frameworks for rapid growth. Nonconservative praetorians see these new theories as more suitable for altering traditional institutions than the old and "corrupt" ideologies of traditional liberalism and parliamentarianism. But the ruler type army also rejects those radical-revolutionary civilian regimes which favor rapid modernization under a one-party system—unless, of course, the latter is dominated by

---

*These percentages are based on African-Arab military elites.

the military—because such regimes are often unsuccessful in meeting the rising expectations they have encouraged. Such behavior does not mean that the officers are revolutionaries; rather, they tend to be reformers. Their sometimes self-proclaimed conversion to revolutionary causes is much less significant than their conversion to anticonservatism.[17] Among potential reformist groups in the state, armies tend to be least radical. As a force for reform, the armies may be adamantly opposed to communism—for example, they may strongly oppose the further extension of Castroism in Latin America. Nasserist praetorianism is also a fervently anti-Communist movement.

There are at least two subtypes of the ruler type praetorian army: the nationalist radical army, represented by the regimes of Gamal Abdel Nasser in Egypt (since 1952), 'Abd al-Karim Qasim in Iraq (1958-1963), and Juan Peron in Argentina (1945-1955); and the reformer army, represented by the military regimes of Houari Boumedienne in Algeria (since 1965), General Suharto in Indonesia (since 1965), the Peruvian Army (since 1970) and the anti-Castro, anti-Communist military rulers in Latin America, such as the Argentine (1965-1973) and Brazilian (since 1964) militaries.

The ruler type praetorian army functions within a left-right continuum of political order. It establishes a new political order in reaction to the old order which it has replaced. Therefore, the ideology of the praetorian army is largely influenced by the ideology of its predecessors. The choice of a new political order is not always easy to make, since often it is easier to decide that a political system should be destroyed than to determine what should replace it. For example, it took Nasser a decade to opt for Arab socialism. The Algerian ruler Houari Boumedienne rejected the radicalization of Ben-Bella's earlier regime.

However, in doing so he has not abandoned Arab socialism; he has merely reduced its ideological intensity and commitments. In this process he has become an antiradical type of ruler; but he has not yet adopted an ideology of his own. By eliminating Ben-Bella's radical legacy he has made a significant move toward the modernization of Algeria.

In Indonesia since the 1965 Communist coup, the army has been in the process of liquidating the old regime, which had been radicalized by Sukarno's "guided democracy." The political evolution of the Indonesian army indicates that, if it is not going to offer an alternative ideology, it could proceed along the lines of a modified guided democracy without the vehemence, the radicalism and the messianism which it demonstrated during the reign of President Sukarno.[18]

Unlike the arbitrator type of praetorian army, the ruler type army does not expect to return to the barracks and relinquish political control when the initial crisis is over. This attitude may result when an important sector of the Officer Corps develops an independent political orientation opposed to the ruling civilian groups. Or it may result when civilian disorganization reaches the point where progressive elements are unable to put their programs into effect. Ruler type officers distrust politicans to the extent that they feel it necessary to occupy formal positions in the governmental structure permanently.

Thus, by the time the ruler army intervenes, the civilians have demonstrated their inability to control the situation. Egyptian officers blamed local civilians for the Palestinian crisis and for the Cairo riots of January 1952; the officers did not even trust those civilians who held political philosophies similar to their own, such as the more radical members of the Wafd or the Muslim Brotherhood.

Capitalizing on the lack of cohesion in political and

social structures, the ruler type army establishes an independent political organization, and maximizes its own rule in order to manipulate the existing disorder. In working toward stability, the ruler type army must legitimize itself by creating its own political party, or some type of corporate group, and a separate political ideology. Nasser's rise to power in Egypt is one of the most prominent illustrations of this phenomenon.

Nasser's political philosophy exemplifies the attitude that army rule is the only alternative to political disorder. In his *Philosophy of the Revolution,* Nasser argues that only the army can meet and solve the praetorian conditions of Egypt and that the army played the role of "vanguard" in the Egypitan revolution.[19]

Some of the extreme radical nationalists in the Iraqi army during the late 1930s took a similar attitude. For example, according to Salah al-Din al-Sabbagh's antiforeign, antiimperialist convictions, it was the army's destiny to deliver Iraq and Islam from the yoke of external and internal oppression.[20]

In 1951, two years after his coup d'etat, Adib Shishakly established a military dictatorship in Syria. By that time, it had become clear to him that the Syrian civilians were too bitterly divided to rule themselves successfully. Most army leaders in the Middle East today express their approval of these military takeovers in Syria, Iraq and Egypt. Several ruler types still act as arbitrators, because of the effective opposition of civilian groups and army rivalry, not because of the army's favoring of civilian rule.

When the ruler type army is committed to political action, it is forced to ignore certain of the traditional characteristics of the professional soldier. As political considerations take preference over those of internal organization and career, professional status and rank may sometimes suffer. A political expert of low rank may in certain situations play a role superior to that of an officer of higher rank. Therefore, the politically involved Officer Corps must develop a set of norms different from those of the professional Officer Corps.[21] Once in power, however, the leader of a ruler type army may attempt to reprofessionalize the military, in order to prevent it from interfering with his policies. Nasser's regime is again the most effective illustration of this process.

2. MODERN EGYPT
1882-1954

The first phase of the Arab world's continuing cultural encounter with the modern West occurred in Egypt and lasted 70 years, from 1798 to 1870.[1] It was characterized by the emulation of European culture and produced the modernization program launched by Egypt's great ruler, Muhammad 'Ali (1805-1848). This program greatly influenced the course of civil-military relations in Egypt laying the foundation for the establishment of the praetorian state which exists there today.

In 1811 Muhammad 'Ali destroyed the old Egyptian power structure by annihilating 400 Mamelukes in the Cairo Citadel, where they had been invited to lunch. After the massacre he expropriated their lands, and began building his own power structure based on a new civil bureaucracy, as well as reform of the army.[2]

The political and military structures established by Muhammad 'Ali were designed both to serve the objectives of his reformist modernization program and to extend his dynasty's power. If his methods were modern, his ends were traditional: he introduced new techniques, not for the creation of a modern state, but in order to consolidate his personal rule.

The power and whims of this ruler not only determined the civil and military administration; he also ran Egypt's economy. "Muhammad 'Ali set himself up as the only proprietor, manufacturer and businessman in all Egypt. Each year, according to the European market, he decided what acreage had to be sown with a given corp."[3]

But, although he destroyed the old political and economic institutions and began the destruction of traditional Egyptian values, Muhammad 'Ali did not create new ones to replace them. He offered no ideology to integrate the various modernization and reform measures he had taken. Unlike contemporary modernizers, Muhammad 'Ali was not even aware of the potential of nationalism as an integrating ideology. In Helen Rivlin's words:

> Muhammad 'Ali was no nationalist in the modern sense and above all no Egyptian nationalist. He considered himself a Turk if anything and thought of Egypt simply as a private preserve to be exploited for his own and his family's benefit.[4]

Muhammad 'Ali distributed the former lands of the Mamelukes in hereditary tenures to members of his family, *fellahin,* and dynastic retainers. Later, the regime actively encouraged the cultivation of cotton and the increasing exports of this product made the Egyptian economy dependent on the international market.[5] The changed ownership, the cultivation of cotton, and finally the introduction of permanent irrigation revolutionized the old agricultural system and resulted, during the nineteenth century, in increasing prosperity for all social sectors. The old feudal system had been destroyed, but a new feudalism replaced it. A few families who owned the large estates exploited the agricultural laborers on their lands. Fellahin were at the mercy of a government which was dominated increasingly by the agricultural interests created by Muhammad 'Ali. With the introduction of Western economic practices and the simultaneous destruction of traditional Islamic moral restraints, exploitation took on a harsher character.[6] But by the beginning of the twentieth century, population growth had begun to whittle down the margin of wealth.

Muhammad 'Ali also reformed and modernized the civil bureaucracy. European standards and skills became paramount in training administrators. European missions operated in Egypt, and Egyptian students studied in Europe. Despite the introduction of new techniques and training in modern administrative methods, the bureaucracy remained a personal adjunct of the ruler, as it had been during previous regimes. In only one aspect was it rational, according to the Weberian model: in the separation of "administrators below the ruler from the ownership of the means of administration."[7] As in the military bureaucracy, Muhammad 'Ali left little to the discretion of his civilian administrators, centralizing control in his own hands. "Every order emanated from Muhammad 'Ali and it is quite clear that he did not let his subordinates use any initiative."[8]

Another aspect of Muhammad 'Ali's general modernization program was the reform of the Egyptian army. The Egyptians traditionally had had a mercenary army. From at least 200 B.C., no native Egyptian had been required to do military service no matter how low his social status, and Egyptians considered this military exemption one of their few precious rights. Until the nineteenth century most of Egypt's soldiers had been Mamelukes.[9] Muhammad 'Ali's plans for the reorganization of the army did not include Egyptianizing it. In traditional fashion, he preferred to exploit the native Egyptian fellahin in agriculture rather than under arms. He intended to create a strong mercenary army of black African slaves led by foreign officers.[10]

The proposed scheme to import mercenaries failed, however; the Greek War of Independence broke out; and the fellahin had to be recruited into the army for the first time in more than 2,000 years. They resented their new role, especially because their foreign rulers did not allow them to rise to positions of command.

Most of those in the military and higher technical schools were still Turks, Circassians and Georgians.[11] When a Staff College was established in 1842, it was reserved for Turks and Mamelukes from Constantinople. Even later, when shortages of men induced Muhammad 'Ali to allow Egyptians to enroll, "they were not allowed to sit for examinations and were given no ranks."[12] This stratification of the army on the basis of nationality left the native Egyptians dissatisfied. The discrimination they suffered in the competition for entering the military schools made them extremely conscious of their identity as Egyptians, yet they took no action against this unjust system.

The self-aggrandizing goals of the modernization program implemented by Muhammad 'Ali and his successors conflicted with the spirit of nationalist revival which the same program aroused among the native Egyptians. Since Mameluke leaders of the Khedivate administration were not concerned with the nationalist revival, the nationalist intelligentsia, who were restricted to lesser positions in the administration, were probably aware that modernization did not contribute to nationalist aspirations. The Khedi-

vate's economic dependence on foreigners further reinforced the view that Muhammad 'Ali's house was not
interested in Egyptianizing Egypt, but rather in establishing dynastic rule with the aid of both urban wealth and
selected village notables. Consequently, modernization in
some sectors became identified with foreign domination,
an identification which later spawned radical-nationalist
movements such as the Muslim Brotherhood.

Opposition to the dynasty arose from the adherents to
each of two ways of life that Muhammad 'Ali's reign
encompassed—the traditional and the modern. The *Ulema*
and the religious sheikhs were devout traditional Muslims.[13] In contrast, the students sent to Europe for
technical training were modernists. Influenced abroad by
liberal constitutionalism, they formed a group known as
the Constitutionalists. In addition to their opposition to
the dynasty, the two groups shared another common goal:
unlike Muhammad 'Ali, they wished to build a distinctive-
ly Egyptian community (Muslim or secular) and to limit
the incursion of foreigners into that community.[14]

As early as the 1870s, secret societies opposed to the
dynasty were organized within the army, in the civil
service, and even within the court, led by Prince Halim and
his Freemasonry group. But the relations between civilian
and military malcontents were tenuous. They had no
common organization or procedures for collaborative
effort. Because the various opposition groups did not act
together, they ultimately failed.[15]

Although the failure of cooperation and coordination
among the opposition groups delayed their political action
for a time, nationalist sentiment continued to grow. By the
end of the reign of Khedive Isma'il, whose ambitious plans
for Egypt's aggrandizement included the development of a
large-scale army staffed mostly by foreigners, national
self-consciousness had risen to the point where revolt

seemed imminent. But Isma'il's deposition in 1879 removed a primary impetus to revolution, and tensions relaxed for a few years.

The 'Urabi Officer Movement of 1879–1882 marked the last large-scale expression of native Egyptian discontent among the fellahin officers in the army before the British occupation. The movement itself was a product of the contradictions created by the reforms of Muhammad 'Ali and his successors. Although the Khedivate had finally permitted the sporadic admission of Egyptians into higher ranks of the army Officer Corps, this reform was short-lived. During the reign of Isma'il the foreign debt had grown enormously. The regime had to economize; hence it made personnel cutbacks throughout the public bureaucracy, including the army. As usual, the native Egyptians were the first to suffer.

In its narrowest aspect, the 'Urabi movement was an attempt on the part of the disgruntled Egyptian officers to obtain redress for their low status in the military hierarchy. Their demands inevitably affected the entire problem of foreign influence, since both the economizing program and the earlier spending sprees owed much to foreign advisors. By now, the significance of the foreigners' influence had touched all sectors of Egyptian society, and the officers suddenly emerged as the "spearhead of a collective movement."[16] Lord Cromer stated that even "the majority of peasants [were] in sympathy with 'Urabi."[17] The officers

> supported the demands of the Constitutionalists for a parliamentary assembly, became mouthpieces for the Afghani partisans in seeking to bind the country more closely to the Ottoman sultan the better to resist foreigners, and ... adopted the slogan "Egypt for the Egyptians". . . . They pleaded the case of the plain soldier and championed the cause of the small farmer. . . .[18]

There was virtually no coordination among the various elements participating in the 'Urabi movement; furthermore, the officer leaders were untalented and inexperienced. As a result, their attempted revolt failed; at which point the British entered and took over the government directly.

Lord Cromer immediately reduced the Egyptian army to a small native force, operating as a branch of the Civil Service. From 1882 until the mid-1930s, the army ceased to serve as a base for nationalists, revolutionaries or modernizers. However, the British takeover did not diminish the significance of the 'Urabi movement as a symbol of developing national consciousness. Although the secret societies, the political officers, the pan-Islamists, and the liberally inclined Constitutionalists and intellectuals were suppressed, as Safran writes: "Certain aspects of al-Afghani's teachings and the aspirations of the Constitutionalists were revived and pushed forward soon after their initial setbacks."[19]

Since the reign of Muhammad 'Ali, the Egyptian polity has been distinguished by its centralized bureaucracy. Muhammad 'Ali made all land and agricultural production public; that is, owned by the dynasty, since the concept of "public" under the aegis of Muhammad 'Ali was actually patrimonial.[20] Patriomonialism is a system in which dependency is based on loyalty and fidelity; both obligation and rule are prescribed by custom and tradition. Weber's description of the patrimonial state is identical with the facts of Muhammad 'Ali's reign: "patrimonial administration was adapted to the satisfaction of purely personal, primarily private household needs of the master . . . in the patrimonial state the most fundamental obligation of the subjects is the material maintenance of the ruler. . . ."[21] In most cases, patrimonial system of government depends on military domination, since political power is considered the ruler's personal property.[22] Thus, the impersonal public does not exist as a political force. Power in 'Ali's dynasty was unconditional, arbitrary and irreconcilable. Muhammad 'Ali's successors, having failed to dominate in the correct patrimonial fasion, were relegated to dividing the dynasty powers and land among the elites of the three new Egyptian classes that developed from Muhammad 'Ali's modernization program. One of these classes was made up of the dynasty, its retainers and the close family clan which owned the choicest land in Egypt. The second group, the rural gentry who had been recruited by the dynasty to serve as its strategic elite,[23] was given land according to title. However, urbanization encouraged a large segment of this class, especially the wealthiest landowners, to migrate to the city and become absentee rural landowners.[24] The third group was composed of former Bedouins and rural notables who had been recruited to various segments of 'Ali's bureaucracy, particularly the military.[25]

S.N. Eisenstadt was one of the first modern social scientists to generalize about the comparative experience of former colonial countries, of which Egypt is a typical example. He clearly distinguished the center level from the periphery; and felt that the dynamics of colonial societies are characterized by an uneven development, "the lack of balance in processes of change and transition that can be found between the 'central' level and the local level."[26]

Center and periphery. On the whole, the roles of intellectuals, scholars, bureaucrats, merchants, colonial administrators and modernizing elites have been centralized in developing polities. Thus, the concept of the center refers to an affirmative attitude toward establishing authority that "imposes the central value system of that society."[27] The whole movement of modernization has revolved around the authority of the center. The conflict between the center and the periphery has been overlooked by nationalist leaders and their modernizing elites, as it has been overlooked by colonial administrators. Modernizing groups have invested greater intellectual efforts, administrative craftmanship and wealth into the center. Thus, in the end, the neglected periphery retaliates. Several African military coups have occurred when the periphery has struck back against the center, while the center, subject to the onslaught of modernization, is itself under fire. Such backlash is not wholly traditionalist; the clash is not necessarily between the center and the periphery, but between coalitions of traditionalists and modernizing elites, associated with the center and the periphery, who are manifestly opposed to one another. Here the military organization becomes instrumental, and its potential as a mobilizing force is demonstrated.[28]

In the nineteenth century, colonialism, both from internal sources (the dynasty) and external ones (the foreign markets and later the British), left their mark on Egypt's social and political development. The traditional Egyptian village continued to be organized on the basis of kinship and buttressed by the tight social control of religion. While the literature on the modernization of developing excolonial countries speaks of detribalization, disintegration of local communities and the disorganization of families, nothing like this happened in Egypt. To begin with, the Egyptian village in the nineteenth century demonstrated no significant social cohesion. "The Egyptian village," writes the sociologist H.H. Ayrout, "is not a community in the social sense, not an organism, but a mass."[29] Egyptian guilds have not been replaced by professional organizations.[30] Independent trade unions never developed by themselves; the first ones were coordinated by the dynasty. No municipal legislation was enacted in Egypt, and when the municipalities of Cairo and Alexandria were established, they were dominated by foreigners.[31] Furthermore, no urban independent bourgeois class has emerged in Egypt, as "The specific structure of Egyptian society has further obstructed the emergence of an independent bourgeoisie."[32]

The modernization of Egypt under Muhammad 'Ali and during the British occupation failed to change two cardinal aspects of that society: the kinship system remained close, particularistic and indifferent to other types of social organization; and the Church and its Ulema priesthood, which opposed birth control laws as late as 1955, remained the dominant ruling class on the local level. Modernization only widened the gap between the center and the periphery. The administrative class in command of change became a new ruling class, an independent landowner group dominant over the rural and urban economies, whose culture, education and status was in sharp contrast to that of the urban and rural poor classes. The political elite was distinguished by its Westernization and its cultural and eductional superiority to the masses of peasants who were not recruited into the political fabric of the system. Kinship and religion were found to be useful tools for dominating the peasantry. The secularization of the center hit the traditional village hard, since the state had ruled local religious functionaries through the central religious establishment. This situation worsened under the military rule of Nasser.[33]

Social change in Egypt was neither cumulative nor protracted. In fact, it hardly existed before 1952. Gabriel Baer writes that

the traditional structure of the family and the status of women did not undergo any change at all. At the beginning of the twentieth century the extended family was still prevalent in

Egypt as a unit of property-owning as well as of dwelling ... the father of the family owned all the family possessions and controlled the family labour-force and its income.[34]

The first legal reforms concerning the Egyptian woman were introduced in 1914. Resistance to such reforms was largely the result of the virtually complete authority of religion on the local level. The vitality of religion and its authorities persisted from Muhammad 'Ali, through and beyond the Nasserite regime.

From the beginning of Muhammad 'Ali's rule to the end of the direct British occupation in 1922, two major politically relevant groups developed among the emerging political and economic elites. One was a bureaucratic, patrimonial, office-holding group, the "in" group of the dynasty; the other, an "outside" group of Muslim cultural nationalists. The Muslim group was basically antagonistic to the regime, although, during its early development, it was sometimes used by the regime. A third group, the urban industrial and service workers, was in the process of being formed. Throughout the British occupation, and particularly during the period preceding 1919, the conflicts that actually existed among these and other divergent social groups were obscured by the unity of their opposition to the obvious imperialism of Great Britain.

In 1919, the objectives of the many different Egyptian groups opposed to the British were embodied in the *Wafd*, a coalition of Muslims and Copts. Its founder, Sa'd Zaghlul, became a new leader of the Egyptian people. The Wafd widened the popular support of a movement which had been organized on a narrow basis for a number of years. Mustafa Kamil had previously attempted to integrate nationalism with liberal and secular constitutionalism, in opposition to the reformist and nationalist Islam of 'Abduh. He established the Nationalist party (*al-hizb al-watani*), which was intellectually committed to Westernization and de-Islamization, that is, to a secular and nationalist ideology. Another secular nationalist group, the *Ummah* party, had been organized by Lutfi al-Sayyid.[35] But while the Nationalist and the Ummah parties represented coteries of liberal-nationalists, civil servants, intellectuals and journalists, the Wafd was Egypt's first mass party.

Throughout the 1920s the Wafd continued to enjoy popularity, largely because of Sa'd Zaghlul's ability to maintain unity among many different socioeconomic groups.[36] Toward the end of his reign, a disparity between the party's declared objectives and its actions became apparent. The Wafd's appeal to the masses began to decline, especially after Zaghlul's death in 1927. By the time Zaghlul's successor, Nahhas Pasha, took over the leadership, the party had become bogged down in the complexities of oligarchical politics. What had been a promising mass party, quickly turned into a party run by large-scale absentee landowners and industrialists.[37]

The bourgeoisie which took over the Wafd, conscious of its own recent origins, emulated the manners and practices of the old landowning elites. Once the bourgeoisie's desire for power was largely satisfied, its members

> used their position to lift themselves up to the ranks of the dominant class by marrying into it or by acquiring estates. This was how the Wafd, which had been dominated at the outset by lawyers and professionals came to be effectively governed by landed interests very soon after. The first Wafdist delegation to Parliament had appeared to its opponents as shockingly plebian; but in every subsequent delegation, an increasing number of members listed their main occupation as landowners.[38]

Thus, the populist trend of the early 1920s reversed itself in favor of oligarchical and clique politics. When, after 1919, the newer and younger nationalist intelligentsia and the junior ranks of the bureaucracy and the military turned to the nationalist political parties, they found them conservative and involved in oligarchical intrigues. The liberalism of the Wafd gave way to a status quo orientation: the only large-scale modernization programs promoted by the party were those benefitting merchants, a few industrialists, and the professional urban classes, including the upper echelons of the military—all allies of the governing elite, and all tainted by the late 1930s with some form of collaboration with the imperialists.

Because of the low degree of economic development and the indirect British rule, the political parties supplied the "native" administration for the executive powers. Between 1919 and 1952 the parties, like those in Isma'il's time, felt their primary role was to channel Egyptians into the public bureaucracy, since neither the fixed rural landowning pattern nor the limited opportunities in industry could provide them with opportunities for mobility. Both this administrative bourgeoisie and the small industrial bourgeoisie lacked the strength and the motivation to challenge the landowners, because the prosperity of the bureaucrats depended on the prosperity of the agricultural exporting sector. Thus, all the literate classes had a stake in keeping the system as it was; and the British occupation provided an additional conservative influence. Egypt's nationalist parties, established as contenders for power along with the monarchy, became oligarchies dedicated to preserving their own limited interests.

Two Generations of Egyptian Nationalists

In the twentieth century two distinctly different groups of Egyptian nationalists emerged, distinguished by the generation of which they were a part, and by their changing attitude toward the West and toward Islam. The first generation of Egyptian nationalists included professionals, intellectuals and the upper middle class—writers, lawyers, engineers and scholars of both Western sciences and Islamic studies—with an essentially optimistic outlook. One of their most influential spokesmen was Mustafa Kamil, who had become known as Egypt's first secular leader during the 1890s. Other leading figures included Lutfi al-Sayyid, Taha Husain, Muhammad Husain Haikal and 'Ali 'Abd al-Raziq. These men had been trained abroad or in European-run schools in the Middle East, at the height of the era of Wilsonian idealism and self-determination. Their optimism was a consequence of their schooling and perhaps also of the fact that some, as members of a privileged class, had escaped much of the oppression from which their fellow Egyptians suffered. Taha Husain expressed the group's view of Egypt's cultural ties in his book, *The Future of Culture in Egypt (Mustaqbal al-Thaqafah fi Misr):*

> The Egyptian mind had no serious contact with the Far Eastern mind; nor did it live harmoniously with the Persian mind. The Egyptian mind has had regular, peaceful, and mutually beneficial relations with only the Near East and Greece. In short, it has been influenced from earliest times by the Mediterranean Sea and the various peoples living around it.[39]

The writings of the liberal nationalists, and of the political theorists allied with them, express the intelligentsia's desire for a resurgence of Egyptian culture. Their essays stress the need for a thorough modernization of the old cutlure, if Egyptian society is to undergo the sort of renaissance required for it to progress along with the other great nations of the world. This optimistic nationalism, dedicated to raising Egypt from the ignominy of preceding decades sought a new level of aspiration—constitutionalism, parliamentarism — a political process borrowed from the West, which would bridge the past and the future, and reinstate Egypt as a world power.[40]

The liberal nationalists seriously attempted to integrate nationalism with liberalism, or at least with some concept of natural and individual rights. They tried to find a common bond between reason and faith to reconcile libertarian ideas with reformist Islamic ethics. At the same time they attempted to create a specifically Egyptian philosophy and national consciousness, completely divorced from any identification with Islam or Arabhood. In so doing, they isolated the Egyptian state from its ideological allies, and thus "made it increasingly distinct from the general Arab movement."[41]

Lutfi al-Sayyid, as a leading member of the liberal nationalists, strongly opposed the pan-Islamic and Ottoman ideals prevalent at the beginning of the century. Rather, he held a tenacious belief in the existence of a separate Egyptian nation. "Our nationalism must rest on our interests and must pursue them on her own."[42] Nor was he concerned with revolutionary changes. In his journal, *al-Jaridah,* he concludes:

> The wave of civilization has come to us with all its virtues and vices, and we must accept it without resisting it. All that we can do is to Egyptianize the good that it carries and narrow down the channels through which the evil can run. We must possess that civilization as it is, but try to control it.[43]

The intellectual strength of the liberal nationalists lay in their shrewd recognition of the revitalizing role of nationalism in Egypt. Their chief weakness was that, although they advocated Egyptianization, their search for a nation-state and for geopolitical and linguistic independence also required a Western rational commitment. As the twentieth century progressed, and Westerners were viewed with increasing distrust, the rejection of Europeanization became common outside the elite group. To other Egyptians, nationalism meant anti-Westernism and identification with Islamic and Arabic groups, if with any supranational organism at all. Furthermore, the liberal nationalists believed that the establishment of constitutional, parliamentary and democratic institutions would be sufficient to Egyptianize their country. They ignored questions of political socialization and economic development, concomitants of Westernization which might have won more people to their side. Here, as in the case of Islamic and Western encounters, political agitation preceded political articulation and ideology in the Muslim world. Thus the emergence of Mustafa Kamil, Egypt's first secular nationalist leader, represents a complete separation from reformist Islam. This new wave of liberal Egyptian nationalism was launched at the turn of the century, by Lord Cromer's modernization program.[44]

Reform, especially in the public services where an effort was made to create a public-oriented bureaucracy, gave further impetus to the secularist wave of Egyptian nationalism. But the first generation of Egyptian nationalists acted as frustrated bureaucrats, rather than as leaders of a political movement. The nationalist movement only coalesced into a political party after 1919, when Mustafa Kamil's agitation and Lutfi al-Sayyid's philosophy fused with the political organization led by Sa'd Zaghlul. After Zaghlul's death in 1927, the Wafd nationalist party quickly became an instrument of Egypt's new landlords. The frustrated bureaucrats and employees of private companies then allied themselves with the Muslim Brotherhood, which was engaged in recruiting the urban middle classes, newly shorn of their influence and power. In this process, the nationalist liberal intellectuals became increasingly isolated.

The primary shortcoming of these early liberal nationalists was their failure to recognize that their ideas needed support from outside their own elite group, to ensure that they persisted without being changed to fit another ideology. Although the liberals planted the seeds of nationalism, there was no other group in Egypt with the necessary social and economic development to cultivate those seeds. Thus, they were able to elicit only a slight response even among Egypt's middle class, the group which was becoming most nationalistic. The Wafd could have captured the imagination of the middle classes but, instead, it became a party of urban landlords:

> In the absence of a definite stand on principles, the struggles between the nationalist governments and the forces representing the religious institutions took place on the level of concrete issues. In that struggle, the governments achieved important tangible successes; but since these were won by the manipulation of traditional motives, the result was to weaken and confuse those concepts, without enhancing, in exchange, the Western-inspired principles and the socio-ethical considerations that motivated the government. [45]

The Fundamentalists

As the liberal nationalists faded into the background of the Egyptian political scene, the second group of nationalists emerged. They were more pragmatic and more activist in their approach, coming as they did from the rural middle class, the product of the upper Nile region's rapid urban growth. This group believed that national independence could be best attained through violence, not by bargaining.

The increased urbanization of the 1930s and the great disparity of living standards between rich and poor, foreigners and natives, were particularly important in transforming the gradual movement of Egyptian nationalism toward liberalism, to a violent anti-liberal, anti-Western activism. Originally a movement involving a limited sector of the urban professional class, it became one which involved both the rural middle class and its urban offshoots.[46]

With the emergence of the fundamental nationalists, belief in Western constitutional and parliamentary methods of government became associated with failure, and was viewed with suspicion. Xenophobic nationalism replaced liberal nationalism, as the liberals came under attack. As is often the case, this reaction was reinforced by socio-economic conditions. The process of reorientation toward fundamental nationalism took place in the context of a political, social and economic crisis beginning in the 1930s and persisting to the 1970s. As the crisis worsened, the reaction to it also grew, so that, by the end of World War II, the whole ideological sphere was dominated by a romantic, vague, inconsistent and aggressive Muslim orientation. This change of direction initiated by the intellectual leaders not only failed to meet the problem it was supposed to solve, but it also encouraged a violent, religious, reactionary mass political movement which was threatening to destroy everything for which liberal nationalism had stood.[47]

The Muslim Brotherhood movement became a major source of inspiration for the new nationalists. At its beginning, in the late 1920s, Brotherhood supporters were clerks, low-paid professionals, technicians and students at both traditional and modern universities. Their numbers grew rapidly from an estimated 3,000 in 1929 to 250,000 in 1947. The Brotherhood's elaborate social welfare system—health and sanitation programs, hospitals and permanent aid funds—its organization of industrial and business firms, public relations offices and similar activities, were all designed to improve the fate of the disinherited. Its puritanism was attractive to many of the more traditional Egyptians, who strongly supported the Brotherhood's campaign against the corruption of the ruling elite by European style night-life and prostitution.

Until its dissolution by Nasser in 1954, the Muslim Brotherhood remained Egypt's Westernizing middle class par excellence. It helped transform liberal nationalism into a force which, although it was fundamentalist and crude, was also ideologically effective and comprehensible, with a strong anti-Western base in Egyptian society.[48]

The fact that the protagonists of Islamic political and legal theory failed to meet the challenge of the modern nation-state remains a burden on every Muslim community which seeks to define its modern political identity.[49] This is not only an Egyptian problem, it was also a major issue in Pakistan. A two-nation theory, invented by the Indian Muslim Muhammad Jinnah, eventually led to the creation of Muslim India as an independent political entity. This fact also imposed upon every Pakistani modernist, secularist and traditionalist representative of this new political entity the obligation to define and formulate the raison d'etre for the creation of a secular Islamic state. Thus, Pakistani leaders from the secularist Muslim League to the fundamentalist *Sufi* were caught in a feverish ideological debate on the future of this Muslim secular state that was separated from the Muslims of India. The Pakistani failure to follow the principles of Islam through an Islamic institution also demonstrates the inability of Muslim legal and political theorists to meet and successfully deal with the modern age.[50]

Since, out of necessity, the principles of Pakistan were determined after its emergence as a separate state, Pakistan represents an extreme case of Islamic modernist failure. Egypt, however, was not beset by the circumstances and conditions upon which Pakistan was founded; it was Muslim, homogeneous and conservative. It had not undergone the same kind of political development as India, and thus the Muslim population of Egypt was not threatened by "Indianization." Both the Egyptian nationalist movement and the government turned their backs on those reformers who were not firm enough in principle and in action to resolve the conflict between traditional Islamic belief and the influence of European culture.[51]

The efforts of that small group of liberal nationalist intellectuals and journalists who repeatedly analyzed the problems of political and secular formulations ended in failure.[52] By turning their backs on Islam, and thus eventually on Egypt's Muslim masses, both the liberal nationalists and the government abandoned the causes which the fundamentalists had used to capture the imagination of the middle class mahadists (Militant Muslim Brothers).[53] Meanwhile the nationalist party, the Wafd, was swallowed by Egypt's new absentee landlords.

The Egyptian political parties did not emphasize the mobilization and organization of an ever greater number of people, the primary function of development-oriented parties in the contemporary period. Rather, they were concerned with manipulating the government for the benefit of class interests. The parties collapsed, not only because their commitment to liberal values was weak, but also because the kind of liberal commitment they had made was inappropriate to successful leadership in a state in the early stages of economic development.

In a society like Egypt's, where classes were polarized and noncohesive, i.e. praetorian, and where neither power nor authority rested with any one consolidated and organized class, the government could not legitimize its rule. Once the potential integrator of the middle classes with other classes and the first nationalist party with a mass following, the Wafd ultimately failed because of the characteristics of the groups from which it drew its support. The middle classes failed to combine nationalist ideology with political power, and thus the failure of the Wafd was also the failure of the Egyptian middle classes.

King Faruq deliberately encouraged the further fragmentation of the middle classes, through policies which encouraged rivalries among his opposition, and within the Wafd.[54] But the negative consequences of relying on the bureaucracy to satisfy demands for mobility became apparent in the 1930s, as the numbers of unemployed intellectuals increased and the condition of the workers failed to show the expected improvement. Each year the ratio of land to population worsened, and dissatisfied intellectuals had an increasing number of potentially revolutionary groups with which to work. The dissatisfied eventually found their champion in Sheikh Hasan al-Banna and his Muslim Brotherhood which became the most popular civilian group in Egypt, next to the Wafd, founded by Zaghlul and the liberals.

The Brotherhood was the major nationalist group of the 1930s and 1940s, untainted by any association with the imperialists and the "corrupt" party regime. It was fervently nationalist, conservative, fundamentalist, xenophobic and antimodernist. The Brotherhood combined concepts of egalitarianism and reform with the tenets of traditional Islam. Groups which were disillusioned with the

Wafd began to support the Sheikh's Society, and the urban *effendi* (rural notables) middle class became its stronghold.[55]

The Brotherhood devoutly advocated a traditional Islamic state founded on the *Sharia'h* (The Law of Islam) and the rule of the Brotherhood as the Islamic Order *(al-Nizam al-Islami),* the "true" representatives of the faith and of the Islamic state. However, aware that the ideal Muslim state must be achieved gradually, and cognizant of the potential power of the Westernized middle class, al-Banna made a concerted and successful effort to recruit adherents to his cause from Egyptian and Islamic nationalists of all types, including both army officers and civil servants. Some, perhaps many, of those he recruited had difficulty identifying with his concept of a Muslim state. However, they found a potential source of political expression in his sytem of organization, with its all-encompassing Egypto-Islamic and Arabic worldview which they could relate to their nationalist aspirations. It remained Egypt's most powerful radical nationalist movement until the Palestine debacle in 1948-1949.

The Brotherhood was not, however, the only radical, antiforeign group. It had a competitor in the *Misr al-Fatat* (Young Egypt), which drew its inspiration from German and Italian Fascism. The Misr al-Fatat was supported by the same social sectors as the Brotherhood—civil servants and army officers, disgruntled by low wages and poor living conditions and humiliated, first by the British occupation and, later, by the creation of a Jewish state.[56]

Like other Egyptian nationalist groups, the Muslim Brotherhood and Misr al-Fatat lacked the support of a sufficiently large sector of the population to win control of the government. Consequently, after the 1936 treaty with the British, the admittance of lower class Egyptians to the military academies, and the lessening of visible

British control over the military, these parties turned to the army for support. This is a first step in the praetorian developmental sequence—civilian intervention in the military.

While both the Muslim Brotherhood and Misr al-Fatat established cells and secret societies in the army, those of the Brotherhood were by far the more influential.[57] Sheikh Hasan al-Banna, first Supreme Guide *(Murshid)* of the Brotherhood, was aware of the importance of the military in inciting violence; hence he planned his infiltration of the army carefully. After 1940, he sought help from the junior officers in Brotherhood programs of terrorism, and also used them to try and win the politically conscious Officer Corps to his movement.[58]

As this civilian infiltration into the army increased, the army was forced to develop political awareness, and to become actively involved in politics. Ties between officers and civilians became more complex, and differences began to appear in the political opinions of the various officers, providing grounds for division among them. The lack of solidarity which originally had encouraged civilian groups to turn to the army for support persisted even after the groups had attained military backing. Eventually their failure to organize efficiently or act together, combined with the growing role of the military in civilian affairs, resulted in the shift of controlling power in the state from civilian leaders to the army. This marked the emergence of Egypt as a praetorian state.

Egypt's military praetorians (interventionists) included many recruits, collaborators and sympathizers of al-Banna whose intellectual and emotional orientation were in harmony with the principles of Egypt's most fundamentalist Islamic movement. A comparison with Muslim Indians is helpful at this point. Islamic fundamentalism was highly conspicuous in an Indian environment. The Muslim Indian secularist oriented intellectuals could hardly compromise with fundamentalism. In Egypt, however, Islamic fundamentalism was more acceptable as a nationalist movement—for the line between secularism and orthodoxy was thin, if laudatory, in the secularist literature. The Brotherhoods' antiforeign and antiimperialist attitudes were sufficient to rally the Westernizing middle classes, both "secular" and orthodox. Its appeal to things Egyptian precluded the type of conflict that had confronted the Indian Muslim middle classes, which had to distinguish themselves from the other Indian middle classes. Thus, to argue that the Muslim Brotherhood was only "a movement of violent reaction against the ideological failure of the intellectual leaders of whatever tendency and against the political-social failure of the Liberal Nationalist regime"[59] is at the same time to account for some of the Muslim Brotherhood's success. The full explanation of Muslim Brotherhood success rests elsewhere—in its representation of Egypt's politically impotent and intellectually bewildered urban and rural Westernizing middle classes.[60]

Historians and interpreters of the Muslim Brotherhood have accepted the convenient description of the Brotherhood as a violent, xenophobic and antirational movement. It undoubtedly had these attributes, as did many other nationalist movements in Egypt and elsewhere. But, after the Palestine debacle, all organized Egyptian parties were characterized by almost daily violence. As Mitchell wrote: "Perhaps the share of the society in the process [violence] was more telling because it was more effective."[61]

The military praetorians, many of whom were former activist supporters and sympathizers of the Muslim Brotherhood, were resolved to carry out al-Banna's social reform through political activism; but only a few were prepared to establish al-Banna's ultimate Islamic state, the Shari'ah state. Social reform among Egypt's masses and agrarian reform demanded that the regime assume a positive attitude toward Islam. Islam was eventually incorporated into the Nasserite ideology as an instrument of identity, a bridge between the rulers and the people, a tool of the Egyptian revolution.

As Egyptian nationalism became increasingly anti-European, it also developed the idea that nationalism must be equated with the restoration of power—that the glory of the ancient Egyptian nation must be recreated. A sense of national consciousness began to develop among the people, and Egyptians also began to see themselves as the historical, physical and intellectual guardians of Islam, which they viewed as the source of their Easternism *(Sharqiyyah)* and identity with the Arab people. When Nasser came to power, he manipulated this growing sense of Arabic and Islamic identity to gain support for his own nationalist ideology. At that point, he intended to incorporate Egyptian nationalism into the wider domains of Islam or of Arab nationalism; however, as a faithful Egyptian nationalist, Nasser subordinated both Islam and Arabhood to his Egyptian nationalism, and all three to his own plans for expansion.

Until 1952, the popularity of the Brotherhood prevented army groups and individuals from taking independent political action. Even the Palestine debacle could not lessen the Brotherhood's power and persuasiveness, due to the increased popularity it won from Egypt's economic dislocation, foreign occupation and the widening of the gap between rich and poor brought about by World War II.[62] In fact, the continuing British presence provided an additional opportunity for the Brotherhood to oppose the Wafd, and thereby strengthen its own position.

The continuing appeal of the Brotherhood lay partly in the clarity and decisiveness with which it accepted or rejected positions and engaged in action. Such clarity was still lacking in the Egyptian army. There are many examples of officers who, after attaining political awareness, shifted among various groups and changed their political positions. For example, Anwar al-Sadat espoused the position of both the Muslim Brotherhood and Misr al-Fatat, at one time or another. Furthermore, there developed a large group of so-called Free Officers in the army. Except in the Muslim Brotherhood cells, between 1936 and 1949 politically oriented officers did not work in unison but rather used espionage and intrigue against one another. Al-Sadat and al-Baghdadi's memoirs reveal the confusion that marked the relations between the Muslim Brotherhood and officers who were sympathetic to its army cells, but not officially affiliated with them. Few nonaffiliated officers accepted the discipline of the Brotherhood; among those who did were 'Abd al-Mun'im 'Abd al-Ra'uf, Kamal al-Din Husain and Anwar al-Sadat.

In 1949, a group of prominent Free Officers formed the Society of Free Officers and became members of the Nasser-Muhanna* clique. Many officers moved in and out of this association,[63] and some—including Kamal al-Din Husain and Husain al-Shafi'i—were Muslim Brotherhood recruits.[64] Although the Muslim Brotherhood had been the inspiration for the founding of the Society of Free Officers, the latter, like the Free Officers in general, had confused relations with the Brotherhood. Before the 1947 Palestine War, all officers, including Nasser, had cooperated in training volunteers for the Palestine campaign. This activity had temporarily improved relations between the Muslim Brotherhood and the Free Officers. However, the Brotherhood did not successfully integrate the Free Officers into its organization. Even its recruits in the army cells, who were expected to play key roles in the

---

*Muhanna was an early conspirator, who disappeared after 1952.

Brotherhood's apparatus for violence, were not well disciplined.

The revolutionary atmosphere which existed early in 1952, along with personal ties between individuals, resulted in temporary cooperation between Free Officers and the Muslim Brotherhood. However, the Brotherhood still did not place Free Officers in its high councils. It continued to regard them as being instrumental to its goal, but did not accept them as equal partners.[65]

In the July 1952 coup the army, led by Nasser, Nagib and the Society of Free Officers, overthrew the monarchy and established its control of Egypt. This marked the high point of political influence within the army, and the establishment of Egypt's praetorian government. While there is no conclusive evidence regarding the Muslim Brotherhood's role in this July coup,[66] it seems likely that the Brotherhood supported it, without active participation. Although some members of the Brotherhood were close to Nasser, the new Supreme Guide, Hudaibi—appointed after al-Banna's assassination in 1949—had to be persuaded to accept the officers' actions.[67]

The political conditions preceding the July 1952 coup represent a classical case of the development of praetorianism: destruction of traditional institutions and values without creation of new ones; increased social polarity manifested in violence and radical movements; impoverished and noncohesive social classes, a fragmented middle class deprived of independent authority and influence and buttressed increasingly by civilian intervention in the army; and the ultimate takeover of civilian institutions by the military. It now remains to examine Egypt as a praetorian state.

On January 23, 1953, six months after the July coup, General Nagib proclaimed the formation of *Hai'at al-Tahrir,* the Liberation Rally, which was to be a "nonpolitical" administrative structure. The Liberation Rally was to serve as the nucleus of a mass party controlled from above; but it actually served to raise the junta from obscurity and eventually outsted Nagib. Like the formation of the Society of Free Officers, the creation of the Liberation Rally was an attempt to establish the political independence of the junta. The rebel officers who then held the Egyptian government, although still operating within a restricted party system, wished to break off association with "collaborationist" parties such as the Muslim Brotherhood, and others who had participated in the cabinets between 1952 and 1954. The Revolutionary Command Council, the Liberation Rally's executive committee, was to establish Nasser's group's autonomy. It was to turn the Society of Free Officers into a governing arm that would dominate the nation.[68] Nagib reluctantly accepted the RCC and advocated cooperation with members of the organized parties who had not been closely associated with the old regime. Nasser and the Free Officers were less optimistic about making the changes necessary for Egypt's liberation through the old, established political organizations. Realizing that Nagib was not a puppet, and that he might join with the parties, perhaps even with the Muslim Brotherhood, and become an arbitrator praetorian, Nasser claimed that the abortive attempt to overthrow his group in January 1953 had been a Wafd-Communist plot, aided by Nagib.[69] On the day of this declaration, Nagib dissolved the political parties.

The Revolutionary Command Council (RCC) then took over the transitional government. The size of the original committee is a matter of dispute, made more complex by the ouster of officers with radical, Socialist, Communist or Muslim Brotherhood leanings, between 1952 and 1954. The Royal Institute of International Affairs provides specific information regarding who was involved in the

1952 organization of the Revolutionary Command Council, indicating that both Vatikiotis[70] and Anwar al-Sadat had erred in their estimates.[71] Excluding Nagib, the Revolutionary Command Council's original membership was 13. Vatikiotis's estimate omitted two of the 13, 'Abd al-Mun'im 'Abd al-Ra'uf and Yusuf Sadiq, both of whom were later purged.[72] Two of the 11 officers he credits with membership in the Free Officers' 1949 founding committee—Kamal al-Din Husain and Husain al-Shafi'i—and a third, Zakariyya Muhyi al-Din, were only recruited for service with the junta the night before the July 1952 coup.

The Revolutionary Command Council became the chief arm of the junta, and of the Rally. Nagib was appointed President, and Nasser Secretary-General. The Liberation Rally then announced a large-scale membership campaign, and the Society of Free Officers, as representatives of the Liberation Rally, moved into Egypt's political, social and economic arenas. The Rally's first attempts to recruit from universities and among the intelligentsia were unsuccessful; later efforts with trade unions and labor groups brought some response. Public health centers, staffed with Liberation Rally supporters, were established, in an attempt to deprive the Muslim Brotherhood of its welfare functions, and thus of its political influence over the lower middle class.[73] By operating through organized unions and agricultural cooperatives, the Liberation Rally reached many peasants in the lower Nile who had never before encountered organized politics, but it did not achieve its goal of recruiting ten million new members. The Rally's pragmatic approach to welfare and education, and its use of the state's power to carry out many needed reforms ignored by the pre-1952 regime, brought its greatest success.

On June 18, 1953, the Revolutionary Command Council officially dissolved the monarchy and proclaimed Egypt a republic. Moving quickly, it appointed one of its members, 'Abd al-Hakim 'Amir to the post of Commander-in-Chief of the armed forces. The army was now completely controlled by the Society of Free Officers.

Despite the dissolution of all political parties, the Muslim Brotherhood was free to operate, largely because the new regime did not feel confident enough to move in on a group with so much influence over the masses. Thus, relations between the Muslim Brotherhood and the Liberation Rally were improved for a time. Kamal al-Din Husain said in Parliament that "the Brothers were among the first in the ranks of Egypt's liberators, whom we have already met in Palestine,"[74] but he made no mention of the fact that Society of Free Officers and Liberation Rally members were infiltrating the Brotherhood.

Purges, both outside and within the Revolutionary Command Council, began at that time. The High Court of the Rally, headed by three Society of Free Officers members ('Abd al-Latif al-Baghdadi, Anwar al-Sadat, and Hasan Ibrahim) tried Wafdists, nationalists and Communists. In 1954, the cabal crushed a military coup. Strengthened by its temporary alliance with the Brotherhood and supported by the transport union, the Revolutionary Command Council decided that the time to strike had come: on February 25, Nagib was dismissed. Nasser, now head of the Revolutionary Command Council, moved to purge all "ideologists" and "social thinkers"—as well as Communists, Socialists and Muslim Brothers—from the Society of Free Officers. Opposition was crushed: Khalid Muhyi al-Din of the armored division, a leader of the countercoup and a Communist sympathizer, was exiled; Ahmad Shauqi, a nationalist, was tried and convicted; 'Abd al-Mun'im 'Abd al Ra'uf, an original Society of Free Officers member but also a devout member of the Muslim

Brotherhood, and a leader of its terrorist organization, was arrested.

With the Society of Free Officers' "left" and "right" flanks purged, Nagib ousted, the army rebels stopped and the parties outlawed, Nasser was ready for the final push in his campaign to consolidate governmental power under the Revolutionary Command Council. His only remaining rival was the Muslim Brotherhood, which by 1954 had formed anti-Liberation Rally groups in Jordan, Syria, Iraq, Lebanon and Saudi Arabia. These were ineffectual, however, and on October 20, 1954, the Muslim Brotherhood itself split apart. The Muslim Brotherhood's Instructor-General, Hasan al-Hudaibi (whose bid for Revolutionary Command Council leadership had been rejected by Nasser), now called for open war on the junta. The attempt by a Muslim Brotherhood laborer to assassinate Nasser on October 26 launched a broad Revolutionary Command Council campaign against the Brotherhood, and in December 1954 the Liberation Court sentenced 19 Muslim Brotherhood leaders to death.

Once in power, the Liberation Rally was faced with the challenge of creating an organizational ideology which would define the military takeover as a just and necessary revolution and establish a core of values on which Nasser's regime could base its claim to legitimacy. A large-scale propaganda effort to this effect began even before the final takeover. Liberation Rally principles were read and explained in places of worship and before women's groups, Boy Scouts and youth groups. The newspaper *al-Ahram* on January 16, 1953, published a list of the Liberation Rally's ideological commitments.[75] The new program included: unconditional evacuation of foreign forces from the Nile Valley; political, economic and social liberation of the Nile people; a new constitution; and realization of social justice—full employment, land reform, and other related projects. The need for national unity was also stressed: "Religion for God's sake, the Nation for the sake of all."[76]

The Sources of Nasserism

The assumption of power by Nasser and the Free Officers in 1952 represented the movement of a socially isolated and politically powerless group from the periphery to the center of Egyptian society. The intellectual and political orientation of these officers was largely determined by their rural middle class origins and also by the historical circumstances of the military profession, which in turn reflected the modes of political organization existing in Egypt under the British.

To get a clearer perspective on the subject, we could contrast patrimonialism (the Ottoman system) with Arab military praetorianism. The types of praetorianism, military establishments, recruitment and structural arrangements that existed in some of the historical empires are functionally equivalent to those in certain developing praetorian polities. We find a valuable analogy in Max Weber's analysis of patrimonialism and praetorianism.[77] According to Weber, patrimonialism, or domination by honoratiores, was a type of authority oriented toward membership in the manorial or the patrimonial group, which was manifested in the decentralization of the patriarchal household and the extension of land holding, empire building, and "extrapatrimonial" recruitment. In this prebureaucratic political system, staff was recruited only to ensure subordination to patriarchal rule, which was extended in "extrapatriarchal" recruitment to relations based on feudal, bureaucratic contracted or merely personal rulership.

In the patrimonial state, the chief obligation of the citizen was the material maintenance of the ruler; thus the military became a permanent fixture as the process of financial rationalization (accounting, budgeting, and so on) developed. Relations between patrimony and conscripts were based on two models: clienteleship and slavery, the combinations varying along with patrimonial rulers and states. The Ottoman Janissaries were recruited among aliens and pariah castes; at other times a "citizen" army of peasants was recruited on a client-protector basis. The feudal armies developed a group of privileged honoratiores, using peasants and military technology. Military training became crucial, and the relationship between patrimonial authority and the military was altered. Here we see the beginning of military professionalism (autonomy, training, skill and so forth) since, at this point, the military establishment could be used against the political subjects of the patrimonial authority.

But, as Weber points out, a ruler whose sole political authority rests on threats, based on military power, ultimately cannot maintain his rule. Weber terms the disintegration of the patrimonial system sultanism.[78] From our viewpoint, the functional equivalent of sultanism is contemporary Arab praetorianism. Praetorianism, as we have discussed, is the institutionalization of the military to the point where it can become an autonomous group, if it is not successfully subdued. The emergence of military professionalism increases the political importance of the military; hence it becomes an autonomous professional organization. When legitimate authority falters, the military fills the gap; in so doing, it fulfills its historical role—that is, praetorianism. Thus, in the Ottoman Empire, the ruling institution became identical with the army during and after the reign of Suleiman the Magnificent. "The Ottoman government had been an army before it was anything else."[79] The Janissaries, the praetorian guard of the Ottoman Empire, were the chief instruments of the sultan from the sixteenth century until 1826. The military became a formidable bureaucracy, growing more complex when firearms and cavalry were introduced. As a bureaucracy—in prebureaucratic and bureaucratic societies—the military was an active participant in politics and, in several of the historical bureaucratic empires, it actually engaged in an independent political struggle.

Modern praetorianism differs significantly from the patrimonial mode in one respect: on the whole, the patrimonial military represented legitimacy; whereas the modern military praetorians have generally challenged legitimacy.

The modern Ottoman army was established in 1826, with the end of Janissary and Bektasi rule. Under the aegis of Sultan Abdul Majid, Captain von Moltke and other German advisors began large-scale reform of the military and the civil service, and opened the army to all subjects of the empire. Thus, the new Ottoman army became a haven for social declasses and parvenus. Captain von Moltke described the Ottoman officer class to two friends on the Berlin General Staff: "The weakest side of the army . . . were the officers. Two Generals in the Army stem from Muhammad Hasai's Harem, a third was only a porter ten years ago, and the fourth was . . . recruited from the prisoners working on a vessel."[80]

The middle and even some of the highest echelons of the Ottoman army were recruited from the lower social classes. Taken when young from family and village, these recruits lost all their original class and social identity, finding new identities in their rank and profession in the army. The Prussian officers encouraged this dedication.

Thus the Ottoman army obliterated the potential radical-ism or social consciousness of the children of the declasses. This made it possible for Arab officers of the Ottoman army, especially Iraqis, to participate in suppressing the Syrian revolt of 1919. This legacy was crucial in the formation of the Syrian and Iraqi armies—all former Ottoman officers. The Arab officer before 1939, according to Be'eri, is heir to the Ottoman officer.[81]

Unlike the other Arab armies, the Egyptian army was modernized and reformed as early as the reign of Muhammad 'Ali. But Muhammad 'Ali, as mentioned earlier, had no desire to make his army Egyptian. In fact, he planned to construct a mercenary army of black African slaves led by foreign officers, hoping thus to exploit the Egyptian *fellah* as a farmer, rather than a soldier.

By the 1830s, however, Muhammad 'Ali's plan had clearly failed, and the army was largely Egyptian, although few of the Arab officers held positions higher than that of Captain. Nevertheless, these reforms did give the army a sense of national consciousness. Khedive Isma'il enhanced this spirit, since his ambitious plans for Egypt's aggrandize-ment included the development of a large-scale army, also to be dominated by foreigners—this time, American officers.[82] In 1882, however, British occupation under Lord Cromer put an end to Isma'il's military: the grand Egyptian army was now a small native force. Reduced in Cromer's time to a branch of the civil service, the army did not become a base for nationalists, revolutionaries or modernizers again until the mid-1930s.[83]

The role of the Arab military recruits in the Ottoman Empire, and later in nineteenth century Egypt, isolated and alienated the Arab soldier from civilian society and from the center of his own society to varying degrees. From the beginnings of the Egyptian army under Muhammad 'Ali through the Khedivate, the Egyptian military was recruited from the periphery, the rural classes. The officers particularly resented this situation, mainly because Muhammad 'Ali's senior officers were foreigners.

In the Arab East, the military was composed largely of unassimilated ethnic minority groups coming from the déclassé rather than the respectable Suni (orthodox) Muslim Arabs. Functioning as a praetorian group defending the sultanate, it owed allegiance to the Osmanli Empire, and it defended the policies of Constantinople rather than that vague, quasi-national entity known as the Arab people. The structure of this military organization reflected the rigid class divisions of the sultanate, and in the late years of the nineteenth century, it also absorbed the rigidities of German militarism. The Arab military was politically docile, an attitude which was reinforced by its German instructors. By virtue of geography and poor communication, it was an isolated group, but not an alienated one.

The Empire was the patron and client of the Ottoman officer. Although he often emerged from among the déclassé he was conservatively and corporately oriented. This orientation is no longer true of Arab officers. After the breakdown of Ottoman legitimacy, their places were filled by nationalists, all seeking a new legitimacy under modifying doctrines: socialism, pan-Arabism, Ba'thism, Nasserism. But their dedication to the military organization still persists. Be'eri observes that, besides Lebanon, the only country with a nonpolitical army in the Arab East is Jordan, with its Legion (now the Jordanian army), which has also been the least revolutionary.[84] The Bedouin (and Circassian) officer in Jordan served the dynastic Hashemite kingdom. No other native army in the Middle East, except in Egypt, has supported its monarchs. Bedouins and Circassians, who constitute over half the

Jordanian officer class, play only a minor role in Arab nationalist politics. The fact that their sole interest is the military organization, and their contentment with the system, homogeneity and rural conservatism, have saved Hussein on at least two occasions. The Jordanian army was not radicalized by Fatah and the militant Palestinians. In fact, the Jordanian army annhilated Fatah in 1970. In Syria, the peasant has been recruited from the agricultural heartland by the "progressive" politicians and officers. The mobility of these officers is the product of the army's independent political action and extreme nationalism. This is also true of the Iraqi and Sudanese officers, but not of the Egyptians.

In contrast, the Egyptian military under the Khedivate was more isolated than alienated. With the 'Urabi revolt, the officers made an overt bid for power, a definite political gesture. The military took an active interest in the Egyptian position, and questioned the virtue of loyalty to a Khedivate that was in debt and subordinate to the British. The problems of the officer class were related to Huntington's definition of professional soldiers:[85] the question of supporting the nationalist-constitutionalist movement as Egyptians or the Khedivate as professional soldiers presented the officer group with a professional and personal challenge. As politically oriented soldiers, it was not possible to remain loyal to the Khedivate, because the Khedive became pliable vis-a-vis the British, and this violated the professional aspirations of the officers of Egyptian Arab origins.[86] But, as the army declined under the British, so did professionalism, and the officer class gradually became alienated, lost all prestige and eventually expressed nationalistic and even radical sentiments. The problem was not merely one of the professional soldier being loyal to the state: it was a question of what type of authority deserved his loyalty. Thus, the subpolitical culture of the Egyptian military and its intellectual attitudes can be traced through the stages of its relations with the Khedivate, the British fiefdom, the monarchy and Egyptian nationalism. A crucial point was reached when the monarchy, in the estimation of the nationalist officers, became a pawn of internal and external imperialism.

The primary characteristics of the Egyptian army which led to its praetorian role, and ultimately to Nasserism, presumably include the army's social context as a déclassé group with the potential for political power, and on its steadily increasing behavior pattern of actual political intervention, beginning with the 'Urabi revolt. These factors represent the opposite of military professionalism, and spring largely from the desire for social status and the will to acquire real power. These ambitions were prevalent even during British rule, and despite the military academy's emphasis on professionalsim among the Egyptian cadets.

Similarly, in developing areas and former colonies, military domination tends to proliferate through the ambitions of new and aggrandizing military castes. As in the Egyptian pattern, these praetorian states tend to limit civilian participation in government and, while identifying with the cause of modernization, tend to restrict it within conservative limits. The Arab countries, which have had vaguely parallel histories, most closely resemble the Egyptian pattern; yet definite resemblances can also be traced to the former colonies of Africa.

The second generation of political reformers were primarily nationalists, emphasizing either their identification with Egypt, or Arabhood and Islam. In its early years, the Wafd had a universal appeal, and initiated a feeling for both politics and nationalism in that sector of the rural population which was above peonage and below prosperity, a group literate in varying degrees but predominately

nonintellectual. Furthermore, the Wafd government decree, following the Anglo-Egyptian treaty of 1936, opened
the military academy to young men regardless of class or
wealth.

Like the other members of the predominantly rural and
minor bureaucratic background from which they were
selected, the first class of cadets under this new dispensa-
tion were largely graduates of conservative Islamic educational institutions, with a general background tending
toward the fundamentalist puritanism of Sufism in religion, primitivism in their attitudes toward Egyptian urban
culture, and an uninformed political activism. Their
narrowly restricted educational background, from the
limited curricula of the Islamic schools to the equally
limited curriculum of the military academy, made them
antiintellectual, since they equated intellectuality with
Western culture and, hence, corruption. In their youth, at
least, they were caught in an intellectual dilemma of their
own: that of reconciling the fundamentalism and puritanism of Islam with the modernizing, Westernizing outlook
of the military academy. All of these young men were
intelligent, and many of them were shrewd; yet they were
limited in their thinking by the narrowness of their general
education and by their professional education as well.
Even in military school, they began to develop a political
subculture devoted to nationalism, Islam and the desire to
use their military positions for the good of Egypt at some
time in the future.

In order to create an independent body of doctrines, a
Nasserite ideology, the Liberation Institute, under the
Liberation Rally Cultural Committee, organized a cadre of
propagandists and writers. The Institute was divided into
four sections: Social Problems, Education, History of
Revolutions and Egyptians History, and Building of the
Spirit. It initiated the *Ikhtarna Lak (We Have Chosen for*

You) series, which included among its first publications Gamal Abdel Nasser's most famous treatise, the *Falsafat al-Thaurah (The Philosophy of the Revolution).*[87] The *Ikhtarna Lak* series soon became the regime's most conspicuous political literature, and the chief source of Nasserite ideology and propaganda for both internal and external consumption.

Internally, this literature was intended to indoctrinate the bureaucracy and the army leadership, especially its middle and junior ranks, with the Nasserite ideology. Some pamphlets, such as Muhammad Mustafa 'Ata's *The Islamic Call,* were designed for external consumption and were translated into English. For the benefit of the senior bureaucracy, selected foreign authors were translated into Arabic, among them Harold Laski, Bertrand Russell and John Strachey. The *Ikhtarna Lak* series grew to include more than 100 titles dealing with wide-ranging historical and political topics such as the Egyptian revolution, Arabism, Islam, imperialism, Zionism, the Suez Canal and social welfare. A special *Ikhtarna Lak* series was written for workers and distributed among the fellahin, and another series was published for school children.

Although these publications represented a new departure from Egyptian society, they were not especially distinguished by originality. Rather than creating an entirely novel revolutionary literature to justify the sweeping changes he advocated, Nasser chose to reassemble and reshuffle slogans, principles and tenets of earlier periods in Egyptian history, making use of those aspects of existing Egyptian and Arab nationalism and Islamic thought which seemed to serve his purpose. To encourage the individual Egyptian to identify with Egyptian nationalism and the state, as represented by the military elite, the ruling group had to use symbols of national identification which could not be separated from past ideas of nationalism, Arabism and Islam. Where no symbols existed, the rulers created them.

The quality of the content of the *Ikhtarna Lak* series was generally inferior to that of earlier independent works which identified the sources of national identity and castigated the national villains—the imperialists and the Zionists. However, for all their intellectual eclecticism, these publications represented an important innovation: they marked the beginning of a state-controlled effort of agitation and propaganda and a conscious attempt to distinguish the Nasserites from the historical nationalists, and above all from the Muslim Brotherhood, and to mark the primacy of Egyptianhood in the Arab-Muslim political universe.

After a decade of reshuffling, the Nasserite ideology emerged, and the Nasserite army elite had truly transformed itself into the political leadership group of Egypt. By 1962, it institutionalized political control and stability by manipulating selected symbols and values.

The interrelations among Islam, Egyptian nationalism and Arab nationalism have been complex throughout the history of Egypt. As H.A.R. Gibb and R. Bowen point out, the problem of how Islam and Arabism, in particular, should relate to one another is an old one:

The imposing Empire of the early Caliphs, so far from forming a unity of any kind, consisted of an ill-assorted group of provinces held together by the military forces and moral prestige of the central government. The community was represented by a relatively small body, chiefly of Arabs, who formed a governing caste in the midst of vast populations which had submitted to their rule. This fact was destined to have two consequences of the utmost importance. It associated Islam, in the minds of Arabs and subjects alike, with Arabdom, and it gave to the form of Islam patronized by the governing classes the character of a state church or 'established' religion.

> The result of the first of these consequences was to place Arabicization before Islamization in the process of moulding the constituent elements of the Empire into a unity.[88]

Arab nationalism comes from pride in an Arab destiny. Yet this conception of destiny cannot be divorced from a pride in an Islamic past.

> The synthesis is close: an identification, at times unconscious, of Islam and Arabism. On the one hand, an Arab need not be pious or spiritually concerned in order to be proud of Islam's historic achievements. . . . On the other hand, Muslim Arabs have never quite acknowledged, never fully incorporated into their thinking and especially their feeling, either that a non-Muslim is really a complete Arab, or that a non-Arab is really a complete Muslim.[89]

Thus the Nasserite Egyptian nationalists reached the conclusion that they could not develop a national consciousness without including Islam and Arabism in it.

When Egypt was semiautonomous under the Ottomans, the first men to express concern for the creation of a single political entity were Muslims influenced by a reformist movement in the Ottoman empire which originated in the Islamic Al-Azhar University. These Muslims were mostly protagonists of pan-Islamism. Conscious of the modernist challenge under the impact of the nineteenth century's rapidly developing technology, their opposition to Western values was ambivalent. They sought to reform Islam, so that it could absorb new learning, but refused to abandon the fundamentals of faith for philosophical rationalism. The leader of these Islamic modernist philosophers was Jamal al-Din al-Afghani. He did not teach coexistence with or adaptation to Westernism, nor did he advocate reforming Islam with Western tools. He spoke of Islam's inherent capacity to absorb science and technology, convinced that

Islam was so firm ideologically that Western science would not affect it. He never addressed himself to the Western intellectual challenge. In the words of Sylvia Haim, his teaching contributed to the spread of revolutionary temper in the Muslim East. Although al-Afghani was a political activist, he did not provide his political movement with a coherent nationalist philosophy. Intellectually, the movement eventually collapsed in the twentieth century. However, its ideology has found new heirs among disgruntled nationalists and Muslims. The Nasserite ideology has an theoretical content which can be traced to al-Afghani, through the Brotherhood.

Al-Afghani's follower and collaborator, Sheikh Muhammad 'Abduh, spoke clearly on the issue of modernism: "We must study the affairs of other religions and states in order to learn the secret of their advancement. . . . Our first duty, then, is to endeavor with all our might and main to spread these sciences in our country."[90] 'Abduh, like al-Afghani, was preoccupied with problems of power and politics early in his career, but his contribution to Islamic political theory or Egyptian nationalism was meager.[91] His real contribution, like al-Afghani's, lies elsewhere, in political agitation and reform. Therefore, twentieth century liberal Egyptian nationalists drew their inspiration, not from 'Abduh, but from Western liberal nationalism.[92]

The anti-Westernism which both 'Abduh and al-Afghani expressed in their writings increased throughout the nineteenth and twentieth centuries.[93] The cultural rejection of the West's ideologies—although not its technology—combined with an increased emphasis on Islam, helped create a common identity among the Egyptians and brought them to reconsider their Islamic ties with the other Arab peoples from whom they had traditionally distinguished themselves.[94]

In the Middle East, only the conservatives believed in

the eternal resilience of tradition and its ability to resist the influence of Western barbarians. Muslim intellectuals engaged in a search for reform to strengthen their creed. Although Muslim scholars were less resistant in withstanding Western cultural encounters, they realized that two possibilities lay open to them: either to abandon tradition and accept change, or to incorporate change into tradition. They chose to do the latter.[95] The Muslims of the 'Abduh and Iqbal schools offered to present, and even interpret, the fundamentals of the Islamic universe, the *Koran*, the *Hadith* and the *Ijma'*, in favor of change.

In Egypt, reformers ultimately failed to meet the challenge of reform. The source of authority in Islam, the *'Ulema'*, could not maintain its status in the face of a disintegrating social system. The reformists, furthermore, offered no ideological or organizational alternatives to a fallen ethos and a disintegrating social system. On the ambiguity between tradition and modernity, Malcolm H. Kerr writes:

> In the past centuries Muslim scholars did not customarily think it their business to reconcile these two sets of contrasting elements (God's Command, Man's behavior). Instead they elaborated their conceptions of the ideal and left Islamic society to cope with actualities by evolving its own practical but largely unacknowledged, psychological and social mechanisms.[96]

This attitude, coupled with the ideological weakness of the distinctions the reformers attempted to make between *din* (religion) and *siyasah* (politics), resulted in the deterioration of Islamic reformism into a vast literature of apologetics. The political agitation of Muslim intellectuals was not buttressed by an effective political organization.[97]

As H.A.R. Gibb points out, the reformers, who constituted a small minority, were unrealistic in expecting to remodel the social institutions of Islam.

The dilemma, real enough though it may seem to the Western-educated middle classes in Egypt and India, is no dilemma at all for the great body of Muslim society. It has arisen in these particular places and circles, not out of an organic revolution within the Muslim society, but out of the superimposition of a different social order professing a social ethic which has never been accepted by any Eastern society as a universal rule.[98]

The modernists were caught between traditionalists and secularists. In the view of the traditionalists,[99] "[The modernists] cannot claim, for all their ingenuity, the authority of the Koran or the authority of the prophetic tradition." This failure of the Islamic reformists widened the gap between the Islamic ethos and the rapidly changing social system of the Arab world.[100] However, their efforts at reform were not entirely in vain, for they stimulated a search for another ethos—secular though it may have been—under the guise of Egyptian and Arab nationalism. The secular Arab nationalist philosophers were not encumbered by the dilemma of the modernists; they dismissed it by ignoring Islam entirely, as a remnant of the past.

The *Falsafat al-Qaumiyyah (The Philosophy of Nationalism),* developed by the most articulate Arab nationalists who inspired Ba'thists and Nasserites alike, made a case for the inseparable ties linking Arab history, the Arab social system and the nationalist ideology—but not the Islamic faith. These men offered the dynamics inherent in a nationalist movement, not a reformed Islam, as an alternative to the traditional ethos. They viewed language and history as the two major intellectual resources on which to base a full and independent modern Arabism. Although they did not speculate, as their predecessors had done, on Islam's inherent force, they turned Islam into a component of modern secular Arab nationalism. Thus, they reduced Islam from a religion to a natural outgrowth of Arabic history, and tried to prove that Islam depended on Arabism, rather than the reverse.[101]

The Muslim Brotherhood and Nasser's Regime: A Comparison of Attitudes

Attitudes toward the West and Modernization. A xenophobic view of Western civilization and Christianity is an article of faith of the Muslim Brotherhood. It considered *al-Isti'mar* (imperialism; literally, "the civilizer") the greatest threat to Islam, dedicated to the destruction of Islamic religious beliefs and values.

Although the Muslim Brotherhood completely rejected Western values and culture, Nasserite literature does not reject all aspects of the scientific and materialistic West. The Nasserites' pragmatic modernizers could not condemn the West for its materialistic ethos, however implicit, since they began by emulating these very theories and models of organization and economic modernization.

To the Muslim Brotherhood, imperialism was basically an anti-Muslim cultural and moral conspiracy, "European crusading" *(al-salebiyah alurubbiyah).*[102] On the other hand, Nasserites considered it a reactionary movement, a form of economic slavery. Imperialism was labelled robbery and theft, a political system of domination, representing the highest state of capitalism. Their view apparently derives from the Hilferding-Hobson-Leninist critique of capitalism and imperialism.

The only area of agreement between the Muslim

Brotherhood and the Nasserites was the Palestine problem: both viewed the Jews as lackeys of imperialism *(rabibat al-Isti'mar)*, denounced the British-American "collective guilt" and the installation of an artificial Jewish state.[103]

Although the Muslim Brotherhood rejected the civilization of the West, the Nasserites rejected only some of its institutional framework, such as plurality of political parties, and parliaments, but not its "materialist civilization." The Muslim Brotherhood called for a Holy War *(al-Harb al-Muquddasah)* against the agents of the West; the Nasserites emulated the organizational genius of the West, especially that of economic modernization.

Attitudes toward Egypt. The Muslim Brotherhood is reformist in terms of religion; it is a neo-Sufist group in search of "pure" and "true" Sufist. The Nasserite ideology rejects the Sufish concept of religion and its leadership; its major appeal is to the select, middle class modernizing intelligentsia. The Nasserites, products of modern bureaucracy, are clearly elitist. However, their concept of an elite relates to an organizational orientation, with a task-oriented type of leadership, while the Sufist concept of an elite is directed toward particularist traditionalistic religious qualification of the leader. The Nasserite elite is recruited from the problem-solvers and the members of the modern bureaucracy. The Brotherhood must recruit its elite only from Sufi militants. Thus, the Brotherhood's system of elite recruitment is more restrictive than that of the Nasserites, even if it appealed to Egypt's modernizing middle classes.

However the two groups may have differed in their programs for reform and change, they held nearly identical views of Egypt. The doctrine of the Muslim Brotherhood was that Egypt was the nation of all Arabs, and the protector of the Islamic faith against the infidels and crusaders; they also felt it was to play an extraordinary role in the rejuvenation of Arabs and Islam.

The Nasserites also have a metaphysical approach to Egypt and Egyptianhood. To the Nasserite, Egypt is the source of light in the world; the protector of Islam and the pride of Arabhood; the noble and ancient builder of civilizations; geographically and strategically the focus of East and West; the center of communication between the Asian and African continents; and the ruler of the Eastern Mediterranean and the Red Sea. (The Nasserites emphasized these themes in their propaganda and publications, particularly during the period of union with Syria.)

Since 1952, the government had demanded total commitment to Egyptian nationalism and viewed the Egyptian people as the vanguard of an Arab nationalist movement. In *the Philosophy of the Revolution,* Nasser dramatizes the hero's role which Egypt must play:

> The story of nations is compounded in great and daring roles of actors playing on the stage of history. . . . I don't know why, and it seems to me that in our region there is a role to be fulfilled, awaiting its actor. Unknowingly so, this role fatigued from its many odysseys in our broad region, seems to finally rest on our national borders hinting that we change our uniforms and act—for there is no other but us who are capable of fulfilling this role. . . . [We must] establish a mighty empire that could rebuild this region and, therefore, give this region a positive and practical role contributing to the future civilization. . . .[104]

Kamal al-Din Husain, an original member of the Society of Free Officers, then Minister of Education, expressed a similar point of view:

> The powerful and glorious foundations of Egypt have no rival among nations of the world. The science and art of ancient Egyptians stem from their belief in the idea of eternity. They

were not satisfied building a new civilization among the ancients. They were determined to spread among the nations of antiquity. The nations drinking from this tasty fountain recognized that Egypt was glorious, Egypt possessed a great tradition, that Egypt was the great power. Has our Egypt of today lost her noble foundations, the rules of its past glory, its strength as an empire? No, no. . . .[105]

The emotional and intellectual commitment to Egypt, and therefore to Egyptian destiny, as compensation for past exploitation, was propounded by Nasser early in his political involvement. "It was apparent to me from the beginning, that our success would depend entirely on our full understanding of the conditions we live by today and our relations to our nation's past history."[106]

Nasser's introduction to Dr. Husain Mu'nis's *Misr Wa-Risaltuha (Egypt's Mission)* bears quoting. Entitled "Egypt as a radiating source of civilization to the world," it reads in part:

Since the beginning of history, EGYPT has radiated information, knowledge and science, carrying in her strong hands the torch of light and civilization to the world.

From EGYPT came the belief of the unity of God, the unified magnificent God, and with this EGYPT shook the ground of every aspect of atheistic beliefs. She liberated humanity from worshipping the stones. . . .

In EGYPT, medicine and surgery were developed which help relieve the sickness and pain of human beings. The first steps in developing modern medicine were the many successful operations by Egyptian doctors.

EGYPT was the ingenius nation which developed the art of geometry and building construction. EGYPT'S fleets crossed the seas carrying knowledge, far out to her neighbors, north, south, east and west. . . .

[In] EGYPT different arts and fields of knowledge flourished. Literature thrived and sculpture and painting reached their peak.

Today this art is still an example and pattern for artists. . . . whenever a person sees the temples and tombs in spite of more than six thousand years, he will think that the artist has just recently finished them. . . .

EGYPT protected Christianity from its birth and has preserved its features and characteristics.

EGYPT chose Islam as a religion—she protected it, kept it, and fostered Islamic scholars who developed new ideas and interpretations concerning the law of Islam Shari'ah and Islamic art.

Because EGYPT sustained the Islamic civilization when it was exposed to crusaders' threats, the Islamic world should express its gratitude to Egypt and consider her as the leader of the Islamic nations.

This is EGYPT in her different stages, the African EGYPT, which lies on the Mediterranean and is the focal point of many civilizations. . . .

EGYPT'S glories in ancient history merit recognition by the world. . . .

EGYPT has kept the individual personality and unique temper of liberal attitudes alive throughout the world. . . . She is the magnificent nation which firmly stood up to the power of the colonizing stream, kept her spirit, personality, and structure.

I don't mean EGYPT lived in isolation and wasn't affected by different civilizations, but I mean that her relations with them were relations of "friendship and love" and she always sought for peace and lived in it.[107]

This nationalist commitment is a major instrument which the junta used to maintain power, bring about political modernization, and promote change. The concomitant modernist commitment in Egypt is part of an identifiable attempt to rid Egypt of a sense of national degradation stemming from colonial rule. Thus, economic modernization has been launched under the aegis of revolution in Egypt. Since earlier modernizing, entrepreneurial and professional classes were dominated by foreigners, and since the literature on al-Isti'mar is still being produced, Egyptianization is defined as modernization run and led by Egyptians.[108] But contemporary Egyptian nationalism is not simply a commitment to modernization. The Egyptian revolution is identified with the rise of the status and dignity of Egyptians. Moreover, Egypt is now identified as the historical, physical and intellectual guardian of Islam; and Islam has become a serviceable source of symbols for the regime, both internally and externally.

Attitudes toward Patriotism and Nationalism. The role of *Wataniyyah* (patriotism) and *Qu'amiyyah* (nationalism) in the doctrines of the Muslim Brotherhood and the Nasserites, and in contemporary Islamic thought, deserves special attention. In fact and theory, both groups supported these concepts, almost feverishly, as a matter of general principle. However, the two groups often diverged in their application of particular aspects of patriotic and nationalistic doctrine.

According to the philosophy of the Muslim Brotherhood, Wataniyyah and Qu'amiyyah are religious duties derived from Islam, and as such, can only be defiled by contact with European influences. To the Nasserites, they are involved with such secular concerns as the promotion of welfare, economic equality and the attainment of individual well-being and dignity for Arabs. To serve these ends, the assimilation of Western technology can be justified.

The Muslim Brotherhood and the Nasserites were in agreement on the primacy of Egypt in the Arab-Muslim world, as a political state and as a pillar of Islam. But patriotism itself was considered by the Muslim Brotherhood to be a duty of the faithful, a religious responsibility, while the Nasserites looked upon it as a duty of the

economic citizen, the producer. Both groups believed that
the nation should be engaged in a constant struggle against
al-Isti'mar, but the Brotherhood saw the struggle as a
moral and religious conflict, while the Nasserites saw the
struggle as a psycho-political encounter, a clash of ideologies. The Muslim Brotherhood viewed the modern secular
state as guilty, or potentially guilty, of shi'k (conspiracy
against the Divine); the Nasserites viewed it as a means of
improving the position of both the Egyptian state and
Islam, in the world as well as in the Middle East. To the
Muslim Brotherhood, the Islamic religion was the core of
nationalism, while the Nasserites saw Islam as a source of
cohesion and identity to be exploited by the secular state.
Egyptianhood, the chief source of identity for Egyptians
and Muslims according to the Brotherhood, was to the
Nasserite the basis for social-political organization and
individual behavior. The Muslim Brotherhood viewed
nationalism as patriotism, as a Qua'ran (Koran) obligation;
the Nasserites viewed nationalism in Egyptian terms, as a
political force depending on Egypt's privileged geograph-
ical position among the Arab countries. The Muslim
Brotherhood conceived of pan-Arabism as the natural
outcome of the desire for conquest and world domination
inherent in Islam. The Nasserites tried to promote pan-
Arabism and the union with Syria on the basis of
establishing a progressive and powerful Arab world state
under Egyptian domination.

Nasser placed Islam in a second circle of political
engagement, in an image of Egypt surrounded by Arabs,
Mohammedans, and Africans. He writes:

> this is the circle which spreads beyond continents and oceans
> which I shall refer to as the circle of our brethren in faith. . . . I
> believe firmly in the practical utility which will occur from the
> beginning [sic] closer to relations between Egypt and the rest of

Islamic states. [Therefore] the Arab circle is the most important of all circles. . . . religion harnesses us to this circle.[109]

Thus Egyptian-Arab antagonism disappears under the banner of Islam, and Islam becomes the bridge for Egyptian-Arab-Muslim unity.

The call for unity and collaboration is one of the most striking features of the Islamic faith. A Muslim is to a Muslim and a believer to a believer, as is a brother to a brother. . . . Disunity is weakness, and dissension is virtually the same as acting against the community.

Islam is called to serve modernist goals:

Arabs and Muslims through the World! Obey God and the Prophet: Unite as one front against whomsoever be your enemy, and give your aid to whomsoever be your friend. Never disagree or weaken, for if you are truly guided by the spirit of Islam you will be the superiors . . . such is not vague or empty words, but they are the expression of my true and genuine feeling. They are words that spring from my heart—a heart that believes firmly and deeply in Islam and its call, the call of power and peace.[110]

While visiting King Saud and making his pilgrimage to the *Ka'ba* (the holy stone in Mecca) in 1955, Nasser spoke to the political significance of Islamic relations:

The pilgrimage should be ranked highest among political powers . . . not as a series of rituals and traditions . . . but as a real political congress wherein leaders of Moslem states, public men . . . their leading industrialists . . . their writers . . . and their youth draw up in this universal Islamic congress on the main lines of policy and cooperation among Islamic countries.[111]

Nasser told Saud of the wisdom of the pilgrimage and of the millions of Muslims throughout Asia, Africa, and the

Soviet Union who could be united through it. "There grows within me the realization of the great potentials hidden in the cooperation of all these Islamic forces."[112]

Nasser was aware of the geopolitical importance of Arabs and of the power implicit in Arab bloc solidarity. The emergence of an independent Arab world forced a practical modification of the isolationlist Egyptian nationalism of Taha Husain and Lutfi al-Sayyid; beyond this, because Arabhood and Islam were made to work for Egyptianization, Nasser used the synthesis of Arabism-Islam-Egyptian nationalism to mobilize all Arabs on behalf of a mighty Egypt *(Misr al-'Uzma).*

Attitudes toward Islam, Economic Reform and Society. The Nasserites cannot conceive of Egyptian society returning to Islam, or of the creation of *Al-Dawlah Muslimah,* an Islamic state based on the principles of the Qua'ran and on the ultimate system: the Islamic Order *(al Nizam al-Islami)* which in turn is based on the Islamic laws, the *Shari'ah.* While the *Shari'ah*—society based on Islamic spiritual and political principles—is unthinkable to the Nasserites for practical reasons, the Muslim Brotherhood considered it an indispensible religious goal. To the Nasserite, Islam is a guide for the reform of society and politics; to the Muslim Brotherhood it is the kernel of the social and political system. The Nasserites speak of social justice primarily in terms of economic reform, to be attained through economic and scientific modernization. The Muslim Brotherhood considered the giving of alms a religious obligation. The Muslim Brotherhood's reliance on Sufist and Qua'Ranic values is opposed to Nasser's belief that the reform of society was the state's responsibility. To the Nasserites equality is an economic value based on a rudimentary concept of a classless society. The Muslim Brotherhood upheld the "Islamic state" as the first step toward the ultimate *Khalifah,* governed by the *shura* system of political consultation.[113] In this state, equality would be based on "personal rights" guaranteed by the shura system. Whereas in Nasser's ideology economic behavior is based on modern economic and etatist functions, the Islamists believed that economic behavior must be guided by social and moral justice, the foundation stones of an Islamic state. To the Nasserites, social justice calls for reform of the laws concerning women and land and for redress against economic oppression. The Muslim Brotherhood's idea of economic reform was limited to the traditional Islamic theme of welfare: the exhortation to the rich to look after the poor. The Nasserites believe that sound economic reform can be best achieved by a modern, organizational, socialized state. Nasserite Arab Socialism denies the right of individual property; all property must be governed by the state. The Muslim Brotherhood stated that property was to be used only by men and that every person had the right to private property. *Zakah* (Alms-giving), the major pillar of Islamic economic theory, is an important part of Sufist morality. To the Nasserites, the pillar of the state is welfare authorized and organized by the welfare state, not as an aspect of the economic indivisibility of man, but as a function of a crude Marxist division of labor between "toilers," "peasants" and "leaders." Thus, the basic economic conservatism of the Muslim Brotherhood contrasts with the relatively radical approach of the Nasserites toward society, economics and politics.

In order to keep the Muslims' confidence, Nasser's state-inspired political propaganda makes reassuring use of Islamic values, wherever possible defining the goals of the praetorian revolution as similar to those of traditional Islamic reform. In this fashion the Islamic commitment becomes a vehicle of political mobilization.

The Islamic Call, written by Muhammad Mustafa 'Ata,

Nasser's chief interpreter of Islam, was a major publication in the *Ikhtarna Lak* series, relating Islam to Egypt. Had it been written before 1952, it would have been submerged in an enormous literature of apologetics. Instead, as a form of nationalist ideology inspired and directed by the Nasserite regime, it became politically meaningful and important. Like other *Ikhtarna Lak* publications, it was intended to provide an intellectual transition from traditionalism to modernity without dissolving the tie with Islam.

'Ata was convinced that the Muslim mission expressed in the Prophet's Call was a cry for reform. Under the heading "Liberation from Bondage," he writes: "liberation of slaves [is] a way to earning God's favor. . . . Islam is unique in teaching that a slave has the same chance of obtaining God's favor as a free man." Furthermore, according to 'Ata, slavery is a Western institution—an "un-Islamic activity." Islam has liberated women by deciding whom they will marry, and it has given "the weak and the poor, slaves included, several opportunities every day to stand on perfect equality with nobles and men of distinction."

The Islamic Call also discusses the problems of poverty. Alms-giving is no longer left to the discretion of the believer, but becomes an obligation; religious festivities must help to alleviate poverty, or at least raise the spirit of the poor. *The Islamic Call* condemns all types of exploitation, and commends group esprit and class cooperation.[114]

The introduction to *The Islamic Call,* written by Nasser, emphasizes the fact that reform cannot be achieved without sacrifice. Anticipating the need for self-denial in the Nasserite era of modernization, it describes the Prophet's life as "one long chain of glorious sacrifices and feats of self-denial."

During nearly two decades of rule in Egypt, the Nasserites fell well below the accomplishments of the Muslim Brotherhood in the areas of social action, indoctrination and communal relations. The Brotherhood's primary aim as a social movement had been the reform of society, education and the behavior of Muslim man in the new era. It established one of the most elaborate private welfare and educational networks in the history of Egypt, as well as the comprehensive mobilization and recruitment of teachers, religious leaders, education, party and movement workers. In fact, in many ways, the Muslim Brotherhood was a prototypical social system, with an elaborate system of education and indoctrination.

Attitudes toward Leadership. Al-Banna and Nasser have both used dictatorial technique of personal authoritarianism, in which one individual becomes the spokesman for a cause: al-Banna, for Islamic reform, and Nasser for the governmental organization he created and for Egypt as an international power. Both have employed the conspiratorial aspects of political groups to capture power; al-Banna using the Muslim Brotherhood as a secret society, Nasser using the Revolutionary Command Council as a cabal.

Al-Banna was Egypt's *murshid* (the spiritual fighter for the faith) and Nasser was its *Rais* (the political and moral leader); each of them using propaganda to create a public image of heroic stature. Through these images, both leaders were made to appear irreplaceable, infallible, wise, perceptive and authoritarian.

To accomplish these abstract, propagandistic ends, al-Banna appealed to Muslims in particular situations—to individuals, families, groups, associations—offering them the religious hope of a revived Islam. On the other hand, Nasser based his appeal on nonviolent concepts: the new

Egyptian-Arab state, the concepts of efficiency, organization, economic reform and the promise of Arab hegemony in the Middle East.

Attitudes toward Political Parties and Organizations. Both the Muslim Brotherhood and the Nasserites opposed political parties, denouncing them as corrupt, irresponsible and reactionary. To the Muslim Brotherhood, political parties and their leaders were a "front for capitalism,"[115] and followed Western patterns of organization.

In the history of Egypt, political parties have become associated with corruption. The view that parliaments and political democracy have failed is now widespread. Another popular view is that parliament requires major constitutional reform. Genuine parliamentary reform comes with the abolition of parties, since, without parties and the presumed corruption of party leaders, life could become compatible with Islam. However, several times during the 1930s al-Banna collaborated with both party leaders and the monarchy. Yet, al-Banna advocated the formation of a single party (the Muslim Brotherhood), to replace the old corrupt parties and introduce an Islamic program of reform.[116] When Nasser assumed power, he also considered parties and party leaders corrupt and corrupting. He then advocated parliamentary reform and sought the establishment of a single party. But there are important differences between Nasser's and al-Banna's ideas of a single political party. Nasser believed in social and political changes via military and bureaucratic organizations. To him there were only two classes: the exploiters and the exploited. The single party must alleviate the conditions of the exploited by creating new administrations, but not parties, for they are "philosophical labyrinths and slogan mongers."

To al-Banna, the Muslim Brotherhood was a movement

whose visions incorporated group interests, and whose tactics represented organic-communal goals in an effort to improve the structure of Islamic society. The Nasserites, on the other hand, projected the future in terms of an abstract technocracy, oriented toward systems, administrative order and depersonalized efficiency.[117] To paraphrase Sheldon Wolin, Nasser is preoccupied with transferring politics from its traditional relationship among individuals, groups and communities, making it a vague function of the corporative and administrative areas.[118] He would turn the citizen into a function, the community into structures, the fabric of society into a web of abstract and corporative relationships, to sublimate the political elements of life. Al-Banna's political movement was designed for purposes of participation and mobilization; Nasser's for those of abstract efficiency and control.

Intellectually, the Nasserites have not improved on the work of their predecessors, but as rulers they were more aggressive, more concerned with political ideologies and more pragmatic. As heirs to Egypt's earlier nationalist movement, they still echo the words of Mustafa Kamil's oration:

> Fatherland, O fatherland: To you my love and my heart. To you my life and existence. To you my blood and my soul. To you my mind and my speech. . . . You, You, O Egypt are life itself, and there is no life but in you. . . .[119]

Yet, their nationalism does not differ radically from that of previous rulers in its method, form and organisation. Nasser has made use of Egyptian nationalism, Islam and Arabism in a pragmatic manner as a means of political manipulation. For him, nationalism has become a valuable tool of the "men of action," those committed to the cause of modernizing Egypt for the Egyptian with as little ideological debt to the West as possible. This need for unifying symbols is still present. Even if it lay dormant after Nasser's death, today, in praetorian Egypt, the drive to develop an Egyptian consciousness and identity is still considered the source of all hope for future development.

3. EGYPT'S MILITARY: A PROGRESSIVE NEW MIDDLE CLASS?

The literature on civil-military relations in developing countries, and especially the literature on the Middle East, exhibits sloppy conceptualization of the relationships among the military, politics and society. Furthermore, the value-laden orientations and inclinations of most authors has both impelled and hindered the development of an all-inclusive and useful general theory of civil-military relations.[1]

The growing role of the military in the new states was explained under the aegis of arching "theories" on "political development" and "modernization." Some scholars on the Middle East returned to an old concept—the "new middle class"—employed during the late 1920s to explain the emergence of fascism. Unwittingly, these scholars used the category to explain the emergence of new military types in underdeveloped countries. This concept was not only used as an analytical tool describing a so-called new phenomenon—the Progressive Military—but also as a prescription for new types of rule in underdeveloped countries.

Among the first attempts at a comparative study of the progressive military in developing states was John J. Johnson's *The Role of the Military in Underdeveloped Countries.* This book presents a collection of independent monographs and also offers comparative, theoretical analyses of the subject by several authors. Edward Shils, a pioneer in comparative theoretical studies, authored the introductory essay, "The Military in the Political Development of the New States,"[2] which sets up the book's theoretical framework. Shils believes that the military's growing role in the politics of new states can be explained by its commitment to modernization and political development. The military is considered a highly effective instrument of modernization by most of the authors in this volume. According to this school of thought, political development and modernization both determine and explain changes in new states. Among the alternative courses of political development is the modernizing military oligarchy.[3] This has become the most prominent model, not only for the role of the military in developing states, but for political development and modernization as well. Following Shils, Lucian Pye, in his essay "Armies in the Process of Political Modernization," argues that the military, as the only organized instituion in a transitional society, is its most modern and rational organization. The military organization, Pye writes, plays a prominent role in the newly emerging nations because it is a modernizing agent.[4]

Two other authors who explain the emergence of the military in developing states as a product of modernization are John J. Johnson and Manfred Halpern. Both feel the military forms the leading stratum of the new middle class. Halpern's expectations for the military in political development surpass any suggested by Shils and Pye. Halpern advances the concept of a New Middle Class (NMC) to explain politics of change and the pivotal role assigned to the army. He divides the middle class in the Middle East into two sectors: the small merchants and the bureaucrats, and the *salariat* (professionals). The latter has the role of modernizer and is identified as the New Middle Class (NMC). The NMC's most powerful and cohesive stratum, according to Halpern, is the army, which represents the NMC as its "most powerful instrument."[5] Thus, the army will help the NMC to marshal mass support: this determines our third model, the Progressive Modernizing Soldier.

This concept of the New Middle Class is the product of work by researchers studying developing politics, who have postulated the existence of a middle class that could and, some argue, should assume primary responsibility for all phases of a nation's development: social, economic and political. Hence, this class has been referred to as the "New Middle Class," in order to differentiate it from the "old" middle class. These researchers maintain that the NMC is more numerous than the "old" class; and that it possesses organizational skills, is honest, develops foward-looking "new men"—in short, that it is capable of spearheading social and political change.

T. Cuyler Young[6] and John J. Johnson[7] cite evidence for the existence of such a class in the Middle East and in other areas. However, Manfred Halpern differs from the foregoing authors in delegating to this class the responsibility for modernization.[8] He sees the New Middle Class as a source of stability, able to coordinate both asymmetrical developments and the processes of social and political change. As others have done, Halpern demonstrates empirically the rise of the NMC; but he also uses sociological and political developmental theories to demonstrate its potentials and its role. What other authors have merely regarded as empirical and "noticeable" phenomena, Halpern raises to the plan of political and social theory, making—theoretically, at least—the rise and the authority of the NMC inevitable.[9]

In addition to demonstrating the emergence and predicting the future rule of the NMC, Halpern analyzes the political behavior of its various class strata and argues that its most cohesive stratum is the army. He goes one step further, asserting that the army Officer Corps has come to represent the interests and aspirations of the New Middle Class and is this class's most powerful instrument. In other words, in the absence of a cohesive New Middle Class, its most powerful instrument, the army, *becomes* the New Middle Class.[10]

Halpern acknowledges that his is not the first work to discuss the emergence of this new class in underdeveloped areas.[11] However, Johnson[12] has been criticized for his vague "middle sectors" concept:

> Everywhere [in Johnson's book] there are impressions, hints, suggestions of the nature of this change [political and social]. What is difficult is the task of raising the social scientist's awareness of the processes involved from the level of impression and suggestion to that of conceptualization and theory productive of reliable knowledge. Johnson refused to accept this challenge, and consequently does not carry the middle sectors from the domain of impressionism to the world of testable theory.[13]

Halpern does express apprehension about possible failure of the NMC:

> The new middle class is faced with most extraordinary opportu-

nities. If it fails to consolidate its authority by achieving sufficient internal cohesion and general social progress, and its factions are instead engaged in ruthless competition for the support of the rural and urban masses, the approaching future is bound to be one of fearful unrest.[14]

Thus, theoretically and empirically, if the NMC does not assert itself, that is, if it neither becomes cohesive nor finds an adequate substitute in the army, if it is fratricidally divided, then these developing polities would be exposed to "fearful unrest."

I will not dispute here the assumption that the presence of a NMC is critical for the modernization and development of a polity. But three of Halpern's assumptions and expectations in connection with the rise of the NMC and its potentials are questionable: the potential cohesiveness of the NMC; the potential capacity of the NMC to bring about social change and political reform; and the extraordinary role assigned to the military in cementing the NMC and enhancing its political power.

The contention that the NMC "has become the chief locus of political and economic power and of social prestige"[15] in Egypt is a reasonable assumption. However, expectations about the results, in terms of political development and social change, of the NMC's rise to political power, are not warranted. On the contrary, it is highly probable that the social prestige of the army is gained at the expense of political development, the cohesiveness of the NMC, and the integrity and resiliency of the army.

Although the focus of this book is on Egypt, which was the first province of the Ottoman Empire to undergo modernization, the relationship between the Egyptian NMC and Egypt's army is analoguous to that in all modernizing Middle Eastern countries where this class has arisen with the help of the army.

A comparative dynamic explanation[16] of the role of the middle class, and its relationship with the bureaucracy in modern Egypt, may help demonstrate why the search for a "new" middle class has been unproductive.

Bureaucracy and Middle Class in Modern Egypt (1805-1919)

The concept of the middle class—with its linkage to social and economic stability, independence, ideological cohesiveness, and its leadership role in industrialization—was developed through an analysis of various West European developments.

From Muhammad 'Ali's retainers, through Isma'il's proxy bureaucratic entrepreneurs, to the political retainers of the monarchy, the Egyptian salariat had never been a middle class in a leadership position. Periods of economic growth under Muhammad 'Ali, and at the beginning of British rule, were not accompanied by the emergence of a strong middle class comparable to that which grew powerful in Europe during the eras of modernization and early industrialization. Stunted in its growth by lopsided economic development, the Egyptian middle class was unable to lead an industrializing Egypt during the twentieth century.[17]

Egypt's middle class is not entrepreneurial because: its first attempts at industrialization and modernization were promoted by the state—first under Muhammad 'Ali, and then under the Khedive Isma'il.[18] Later, the entrepreneurial functions were taken up by foreigners; native Egyptians, having no experience, found it difficult to compete, and those who wanted to climb the socioeconomic ladder traditionally preferred bureaucratic and administrative positions.

Gabriel Baer presents a further reason for Egypt's failure to develop independent entrepreneurs and a creative middle class in the European sense—the characteristic Egyptian guild system.[19] Gibb and Bowen had established that the characteristic feature of the social organization of towns, and the core of the medieval Islamic culture, was the guild or corporation *(ta'ifah).*[20] Baer writes:

> Even if Muhammad 'Ali's "industrial revolution" or his so-called "complete transformation of the way of production" affected the artisan guilds ... and their members ... it was mainly foreign trade which Muhammad 'Ali monopolized, and it was mainly the fellahs whom he recruited, not the townspeople. In any case, the establishment of his industries as such did not affect the overwhelming majority of the guild members, who did not even have any contact with the new factory workers.[21]

Muhammad 'Ali, in trying to integrate Egypt "as an agricultural unit in the world-wide economic system"[22] despite a shortage of agricultural labor,[23] concentrated his efforts on land improvement and on the fellahin as agricultural workers. However, as Baer conclusively demonstrates, Ali did not destroy the guilds. Merchant and transport guilds were not harmed by 'Ali's policies; some guild members were even recruited into the army and worked for the government.[24] In fact, Baer argues, Muhammad 'Ali harnessed the guild corporative system for his own purposes, and thus many governmental and bureaucratic functions in industry and trade were carried out by guild members:

> Since the government was unable to replace them [the guilds] by a new modern administrative system, it had to keep them

intact in order to fulfill a number of important public functions.[25]

The guilds supplied labor; they arbitrated their own disputes; and the Shaykhs, as heads of the guilds, were responsible for collecting revenue from guild members.[26]

The preservation of the guilds employed "the whole gainfully occupied town population except the higher bureaucracy, the army, and the 'Ulema'."[27] Thus, except for the latter and the guild members, the entire urban population was in government employ, advancing Muhammad 'Ali's modernization program.[28] But what Muhammad 'Ali really wanted was to establish his own dynasty, including all of Egypt, and perhaps the entire Ottoman Empire as well. He realized that he needed to transform Egypt, which he did by sustaining the guilds, and thus supporting the corporate system. This, in turn, helped Ali to use the fruits of Egypt's modernization for his own dynastic purposes.

The government did not intervene in society's urban economic structure—a policy that had crucial consequences for industrialization.

> This period, 1816-1840, saw Muhammad 'Ali in a great effort to achieve independence and empire, gather into his hands all the productive resources of Egypt and with indomitable will impose upon the people an almost incredible effort of development. To his ownership of all the land of the country, Muhammad 'Ali added the ownership of all the agricultural and manufactured products by declaring one after another of them government monopolies.[29]

'Ali's industrialization program also extended government control over industry:

The existing industries were decreed government monopolies. The system of industry was not changed, the artisans remained in their workshops and kept their machines, but they had to take their raw materials from the government and deliver to the government their finished products at prices imposed by the government.[30]

Such a system of modernization was hardly conducive to the growth of independent entrepreneurs, or of a creative middle class.

In a reaction against Egyptian capitalists, a number of Muhammad 'Ali's factories were liquidated and sold by his successors, 'Abbas and Sa'id, who also discouraged other forms of capitalism.[31] Baer enumerates "two important factors" that discouraged investment in industry, and were responsible for the subsequent decline of Egyptian capitalists: the memory of Muhammad 'Ali's discriminatory policies and government control; and the great risk for the small Egyptian market of investing in industry. Investment in agricultural land was considered a better risk, as it was potentially more profitable.[32] Thus, Baer concludes that "after the failure of Muhammad 'Ali's industrial experiment, no serious industrial development took place in Egypt for decades."[33] Another factor related to the decline of Egyptian industry during Muhammad 'Ali's regime was his mistake in hoping for immediate returns and great profit in industry. "In this he was deceived," writes Crouchley. "Far from being a source of profit, the industries were a drain of money and expense as long as they continued to exist."[34]

In addition to government monopolies in industry and agriculture, the British occupation further discouraged industrialization in Egypt. The British authorities were against industrialization, generally. Furthermore, Lord Cromer's land reforms created an absentee landlord class, which further reinforced the already conservative nature of the country's ruling class. During the British era, the middle class was largely composed of foreigners. Thus there was no true Egyptian middle class.

Muhammad 'Ali, himself a foreigner (an Albanian Ottoman officer), laid the foundation for modernizing the Egyptian bureaucracy when he established a large, dependent bureaucracy to carry out his reformist and empire-building plans. One of his central points of reform was the agricultural system; he emancipated the fellah, as the fellah's Prussian counterpart had been emancipated—not for liberal reasons, but to ensure the ruler's and his dynasty's power. Essentially, Muhammad 'Ali was trying to raise the fellah to the level of an acceptably efficient producer. In conjunction with these other policies, Muhammad 'Ali began a revolution in land tenure, by abolishing the tax on farming. But he also granted large estates to his relatives. Thus, the effect of Muhammad 'Ali's changes was the improvement of both the fellah's position and that of the large landlord.

With Muhammad 'Ali's death, Egyptian rulers became dependent upon the bureaucracy he had created. And, while this bureaucracy was no longer completely subservient to Egypt's rulers, the Khedive continued to dominate the bureaucracy by attempting to coerce the bureaucracy through intrigue and espionage. Muhammad 'Ali had used these practices to completely dominate the political management of Egypt. Because his heirs lacked his talent for manipulation, they were forced to share the political management of the country with the bureacracy.

The resulting absence of industrialization and entrepreneurial initiative, and the concern for the formation of a nationalist bourgeoisie, had significant social and political implications. Of the world's second generation industrialized nations, Germany and Japan are most like Egypt. David Landes has pointed out that neither Germany nor Japan could have developed or industrialized without the reform politics of their modernizing elites.[35] The nation, and especially its bureaucracy, was considered above local, regional and even class interests. Furthermore, political leadership in both Germany and Japan emerged from conservative and economically backward groups—the Junkers (warrior class) in Prussia and the Satsuma-Choshu (tribal domain) in Japan. In neither country was reform launched by the economically developed and liberal middle classes, because these middle classes could not begin to rival the power of the agrarian ruling classes of East Prussia and Satsuma-Choshu. In both countries the traditional ruling groups sought new bases of economic and political power. Thus, in Prussia, an "alliance" was formed between the peasantry and the Junker bureaucracy. Eventually, the Junker bureaucracy came to dominate the landed Junkers.[36] In Japan, the samurai (warrior class), with little loyalty to land and class, identified the Meiji Restoration (1807-1868) with the nation. Both groups eventually became aware that reform was slowly eroding their power, but by then it was too late.

By successfully managing economic modernization, and inspired by nationalism, the bureaucracies in Prussia and Japan eventually came to serve the public, even if that "public" was sometimes limited to Prussian Junkers and the Meiji oligarchy. As it achieved legal autonomy and nationality (in the Weberian sense), bureaucracy gradually widened the scope of political management. In Egypt, however, the bureaucracy was not transformed into an autonomous political structure. Nor were the national procedures introduced by Muhammad 'Ali institutionalized.

The growth of an independent and powerful land-ownership class in Egypt was a consequence of Muhammad 'Ali's unfinished modernization policies. As pointed out earlier, investors preferred agricultural land over industry. And Muhammad 'Ali's successors lacked his genius for controlling conflicting bureaucratic systems—patrimonial and rational. Thus, bureaucracy began to serve itself rather than the dynasty. Muhammad 'Ali's policy of state monopoly over agricultural land and his tight control over landowners and fellahs was reversed under Taufiq, during the latter part of the nineteenth century. And, with the development of finance capital,[37] Muhammad 'Ali's successors increased the power of independent landowners. Thus Muhammad 'Ali's system of modernization and state control was completely reversed, so that bureaucracy no longer served Muhammad 'Ali's dynastic aims as it had in the early part of the nineteenth century, but rather enhanced the increasing power of the absentee rural landlords who dominated politics, finance and administration.[38]

The landowning classes swelled as the bureaucrats of Muhammad Ali's successors manipulated their offices so as to become landowners. Muhammad 'Ali had used intrigue as a technique to control his bureaucracy, but his lesser heirs, when bidding for the power of bureaucrats, rewarded them with land titles. Thus, politics became the means of securing land and offices from the dynasty, as Muhammad 'Ali's personal tyranny was replaced by the smaller tyrannies of office seekers and landowners.

Thus, the entrepreneurial and reformist efforts charac-teristic of 'Ali's dynasty were later channeled into efforts to divide his land among competing bureaucrats turned landowners. The failure of Muhammad 'Ali's successors to institutionalize an independent bureaucracy turned the bureaucratic structure into an instrument of political and economic patronage for the few and the powerful.

The NMC: Theory, Assumptions, Potentials

Although he is aware of the differences between the European and Middle Eastern middle classes, Morroe Berger still seems to believe that economic growth in the Middle East could give the middle classes (including Egypt's) a role similar to that played by the Western European middle classes. He writes:

> If the economic growth can open up new [avenues of social mobility] and if new social groups can acquire a stake in continued economic advance and in the sharing of political power, the Middle East may well enter a period of greater social and political stability. The middle class can play a limited but important part in such changes, especially by its example; through its flexibility and its familiarity with the new patterns, and its close relationship with those elements of the population that want to cling to the old. If the various types of elite groups in the middle class can develop a spirit of independence and of responsibility to the entire society rather than only to their own narrow and immediate interests, they may be able to provide a good measure of leadership that may take some parts of the Arab world into a new era of spiritual and political development as well as of economic growth.[39]

The number of "ifs" in this argument indicates the extent to which Berger is still reasoning on the basis of Western European experience. With the "ifs" met, the middle class, in a sense, can come into its own. Berger does not argue for a similar capitalistic development in Egypt;

but he does see the Egyptian middle class as the potential, although limited, consolidator of the state.

Berger divides the Middle Eastern middle class into two sectors: first, the merchants and small manufacturers "whose income and influence are not great enough to place them among the really powerful men in political and economic life";[40] and second, a mixed group of independent professionals and employed bureaucrats. Although he does not specify which of the two "has had enormous influence as a vehicle of modernization and introduction of Western elements into the Arab world,"[41] it seems likely that he means both groups. However, Halpern assigns this innovative function to the second group alone, that is, to the salariat, which he identifies as the new middle class.[42] Halpern says:

> The new middle class has been able to act as a separate and independent force because: (1) prior to its seizure pf power, it is freer than any other class from traditional bonds and preconceptions, and better equipped to manipulate armies and voluntary organizations as revolutionary political instruments; (2) once it controls the machinery of a modernizing state, it possesses a power base superior to that which any other class in the Middle East can muster on the basis of prestige, property, or physical force; (3) it is numerically one of the largest groups within the modern sector of society; (4) it is, so far, more obviously cohesive, more self-conscious, and better trained than any other class; (5) its political, economic, and social actions, in so far as they come to grips with social change, are decisive in determining the role other classes will play in the future; and (6) it has shown itself capable of marshalling mass support.[43]

This brings us to the fundamental problem of defining "class." Obviously, social is related to social stratification. And any stratification system depends upon the value system of the society in which it functions. Can the New

Middle Class be distinguished from the "old" one on the basis of values, or its members' occupations? One could say that both the "old" and the "new" middle classes are interested in status, order, security, prosperity and property. Then, what is the difference between the NMC and the "old" middle class? The scale of stratification must follow the continuum of order in both the old and the new middle classes. And the New Middle Class, if it is not identified by economics (or occupations), must be identified by something else. Thus, what is "new" about this class is its capacity to create political order. However, nowhere has Halpern convinced us that the New Middle Class *has* created a new order. Thus far, in fact, the New Middle Class has only succeeded in undermining the old order—or, rather, in toppling it in the last stages of its decay. The New Middle Class has established no alternative, stable, visible or even hypothetical new order in Egypt, elsewhere in the Middle East or in Africa.

The fundamental question is which strata belong to the NMC and which are excluded, since we must use a categorical definition of class as the holding of common positions along an economic or other continuum—such as modernization, change or new order. Employing this definition, it becomes rather difficult to decide which strata belong to the New Middle Class, or for that matter, to any other "new" class. For here we do not have the uniform and relational continuity between the strata which normally marks a class. If we pursue a classical definition of class, such as Marx's economic definition, or Weber's one based on status, we must still cluster the strata along a certain continuum. If the continuum is as amorphous as "expectations for modernization," and the strata are defined as belonging by virtue of their common ideas, actions and careers, that would suggest that Johnson's middle sectors, or Berger's middle class, fit the new middle class better than does Halpern's own definition. After all, a class must operate as a class, however uncohesive and weak its composite strata may be, so long as its major stratum dominates. The difference between mechanical stratification and class is the latter's uniformity along a clearly defined continuum. The different strata must collaborate, cooperate with one another in certain actions. Taking modernization as a continuum, one is using an amorphous concept which has not yet been clearly defined anywhere in the literature.

We must ask the following questions: What is the style of this new middle class collaboration? And how do we measure collaboration and cohesion, especially along such a vague continuum as modernization? If common ideas or careers are important criteria of new middle class membership, it seems likely that a differential such as the distribution of prestige should precede class action. The test is therefore status increment by class cohesion—"belonging to modernization" as Halpern and company would have it. If a characteristic of the New Middle Class is its adherence to modernization and order, what guarantees the NMC's cohesiveness? In fact, adherence to modernization and order, as we shall demonstrate later, is the chief obstacle to the development of the NMC.

Halpern is simply talking about a typology of elite circulation, a concept which cannot predict which elite will rule now and which one will rule later. The theory of the new middle class should have explained or predicted at least one of the preceding coalitions. Why do we need a new theory that adds little to old explanations and fails to explain new situations? Could the theory of the new middle class explain, for instance, what type of palatial, governmental and institutional combinations Nasser would have preferred after his disastrous defeat of 1967? Would Nasser have made an alliance with the army against the

Arab Socialist Union, with the Arab Socialists against the army? Would we have made an alliance with the army, the Arab Socialist Union functionaries, and the students; or would he have encouraged rivalry among all these groups, to enhance his power? Would he have encouraged the kind of palatial intrigue and counterintrigue on which the Egyptian regime has thrived from 1952 to 1968? Or would he have chosen a new type of social revolution, which would involve the masses and would no longer depend upon the so-called "representatives" of workers and peasants, who are only the functionaries of the Arab Socialist Union? Did Nasser, the most prominent representative of the NMC, differ politically from the old middle class in his views of the peasants, the unskilled workers, the bureaucracy and the intellectuals?

The concept of a new middle class is hardly new. In 1926, Professors Emil Lederer and Jakob Marschak[44] developed the idea of a new middle class *(Neuer Mittelstand)*, involving social scientists in a formidable debate. According to Lederer and Marschak, the new middle class comprised the salaried employees and industry-paid salariat. An analysis of the weaknesses of the new middle class yields an occupational salad of salaried employees, from post office clerks to senior executives. Neither identifying them as a class nor, certainly, as a new middle class. On the basis of Lederer and Marschak's work, Ralf Dahrendorf concludes that the structure of this "new middle class" has resisted all attempts to define its upper and lower limits.[45] The NMC is not an independent class; some of its strata are part of the "old" middle class and others do not make a basis for a new economic class. Thus, the broad definitions of Berger and Johnson are not suitable for explaining the political behavior of a new middle class. Why create an artificial class from several disparate strata of the middle class? If the Middle Eastern middle classes were broad and variegated—that is, if over 20 percent of the male labor force were employed in commerce, banking, finance, technical, administrative and clerical work—then it would be meaningful for us to stratify it into groups based on factors other than occupation. The confusion grows when we ask whether the NMC is a ruling class or a working class.

After all, if we cannot define the upper and lower limits of the New Middle Class, then how do we know what group we are talking about? Is it a ruling class that we can describe in terms of salary, status and position vis-a-vis modernization, in the expectation that a new order would legitimize this class in power? Or, are we talking about a group which we could call a working class, a group whose concern and interest is purely economic?[46] Obviously, without an economic continuum of class, the New Middle Class becomes a confusing concept. Apparently the only way to identify this class is on an economic-status basis.

In terms of prestige and income, many salaried employees occupy a position somewhere between the very wealthy and the very poor, in the middle of the scale of social stratification. But in a situation of social and political conflict—whether conflict is defined in Marxian or other terms—this kind of intermediate position does not exist. Michael Crozier notes:

> The situation of the salaried employee is one that makes possible an identification with the world of the ruling class and promises considerable rewards if this suceeds. But at the same time it is a working-class situation and therefore suffers from most of those limitations to which all other workers are subjected—limited income as well as lack of autonomy and a position of subordination.[47]

The members of Halpern's New Middle Class—supposedly defined by its ideas, actions and careers vis-a-vis modernization—are really Lederer, Marschak and Crozier's middle echelon bureaucrats. Halpern dismisses an economic definition of class in favor of one based on class as order-maker. If we can discern and demonstrate the fulfillment of New Middle Class expectations, then we may have a criterion to distinguish "old" from "new" middle classes. But Halpern's argument fails on precisely this point, and it is here that his assumptions may be challenged and the argument made that the new class is useless as an explanation of the politics of change in the Middle East or elsewhere. Those strata which belong to the New Middle Class are nothing but new elites clustered around, and probably created by, modernization. They have not cut themselves off from their middle-class origins or expectations.

Thus, the theory of the New Middle Class does not explain social change. At best, it can only explain patterns of conflict over political power within the strata of the middle class.

The most feasible way to use information on status increment is to analyze the effects of status improvements on economic and occupational positions and political orientations. In other words, role relationships are the fundamental criteria by which one assigns a particular stratum to a particular class. The concept of role could be more useful than the concept of a New Middle Class in explaining change in developing countries.

The decomposition of labor and capital has been the result of social developments that have occurred since Marx, but the "new middle class" was born *decomposed* [italics mine]. It neither has been nor is it ever likely to be a class in any sense of this term. But while there is no "new middle class," there are, of course, white collar workers and bureaucrats, and the growth of these groups is one of the striking features of historical development in the past century. What is their effect on class structure and class conflict, if it is not that of adding a new class to the older one Marx described. It follows from our analysis that the emergence of salaried employees means in the first place an extension of the older classes of bourgeoisie and proletariat.[48]

If we accept the above analysis of Dahrendorf's thesis, then we find Halpern's book useful. Halpern explains throughout his book that salaried employees emerged as an extension of the older classes of bourgeoisie and skilled proletariats. And if one rejects explanations of class that are Marxist, economic and sociological, one might choose Dahrendorf's explanation instead. For all intents and purposes, the salariat is not a new breed of the old bourgeoisie, but another extension of this class; thus it probably suffers from the same weaknesses as its predecessor.

The Army as the Instrument of NMC Cohesion

According to Halpern, the military is the most cohesive stratum of the NMC, and the NMC is "as least" represented by the army when the army is "securely anchored in a well-organized movement."[49] He also believes that the NMC's success in marshalling mass support depends on the army, its most powerful instrument.[50] The military plays an extraordinary role as the consolidator of the NMC because it has "served as national standard-bearer when others who claimed that role proved irresponsible and ineffective."[51] The army has been propelled into the political arena by its organization and, compared with the rest of the society, modernized early. Consequently, "the more the army was modernized, the more its composition [and] organization, spirit, capabilities, and purpose con-

stituted a radical criticism of the existing political system."[52] Halpern summarizes his argument:

> Within the army, modern technology was eagerly welcomed and
> its usefulness and power appreciated. By contrast, the political
> system showed greater inertia, inefficiency, skepticism, and greed
> in utilizing the products of modern science. Within the army,
> merit was often rewarded. In civilian politics, corruption,
> nepotism, and bribery loomed much larger. Within the army, a
> sense of national mission transcending parochial, regional or
> economic interests, or kinship ties seemed to be much more
> clearly defined than anywhere else in society.[53]

But the acceptance of this new class as potentially
cohesive and the expectation of the coming consolidation
of all new middle class strata under the auspices of the
army are not convincing. Still less convincing is the
identification of the NMC as an intelligentsia.[54] "The
intelligentsia is the predominant force of this class"
because "it originates in the intellectual and social transformation of Middle Eastern society" and therefore "its
various strata consist of new men who intervene in the
process of modernization and hence assume additional
roles in modernization."[55] In military-dominated politics,
neither the civilian nor the military stratum tends to be
cohesive. Furthermore, the dynamics of transformation are
more likely to increase division among the NMC strata,
than to produce consolidation. For example, recent
transformation of the Egyptian and Syrian societies has
increased conflicts among their NMC strata, and intensified
the brutal internal struggle for power and primacy.
Apparently Halpern's new class is similar to Karl Mannheim's "socially unattached intelligentsia" (*Freisch-
webende intelligenz*).[56] That is, Halpern feels that the
NMC strata have become a class because they are potential-

ly cohesive. Mannheim admits that this intelligentsia is not homogeneous, although it has absorbed a common world-view and a readiness for action. But homogeneity and a common worldview alone are not sufficient conditions for cohesiveness and common action.

The political histories of Egypt since 1952, Syria since 1949, and Iraq since 1958 demonstrate that neither the new middle class nor the army are—even potentially—one social, ideological or political class. Therefore, social scientists would do well to concentrate on the complex-ities and divisions within the stratification system of each stratum of the NMC.

It may, indeed, be more relevant to identify the lines of potential conflict, than those of potential cohesion. Halpern does see the problem of internal conflict, but he does not use it as the key to his analysis. He writes:

> The army in politics cannot become an institution above the battle. It intervenes as a partisan, representing a new class with whom the majority in the country does not yet share a common consciousness. It is itself a most sensitive mirror of internal conflicts, within the new middle class. . . . It will be unable to avoid factionalism within the ruling junta unless the whole junta or its dominant faction, is securely anchored in a well-organized movement representing at least the new middle class.[57]

Halpern's observation that the 1952 military coup in Egypt was without violence,[58] and that a new social class displaced the landed ruling class, indicates the political apathy of the population; at the time of the coup this apathy could be found even in the army, and certainly in parts of the New Middle Class. Such apathy was typical of the "palatial intrigue" politics of a state dominated by feudalism—politics in which Nasser and the Free Officers played an important part between 1945 and 1952. When, in 1954, the army finally became "securely anchored," this did not demonstrate the ideological convictions of a new class or a new intelligentsia. Only in 1961 did Nasser finally opt for a socialist system. "Ten years after the revolution of 1952 the Egyptian free-enterprise system had been effectively transformed into a centrally-controlled economy."[59] Even today, the Egyptian army has not established "a well organized movement." The concept of the New Middle Class is plagued by all of the problems that the earlier concept of the middle classes encountered.

As Halpern has suggested, army rule in the Middle East has resulted in neither social stability nor mass political participation. In Syria and Iraq, the army has been responsible for the regime's political instability; in Egypt, recent political stability is a product of traditional political apathy, political coercion and a dependent bureaucracy, rather than of consolidation of social and political groups. The newly acquired prestige of Egypt's officer class has made the rest of this new class presented by Halpern not more cohesive, but merely more dependent.

Middle Eastern military officers are the products of modern organizations, more so than the rest of the population. Their values and orientations are modern, and they use modern tools and techniques. But their attitudes reveal little about their ability to transfer these characteristics to civilian society. Such transfer requires leadership qualities, particularly political ones. Are military qualities—Halpern calls them "skills"—of honesty, ability and decisiveness, identical with political leadership skills? The fratricidal Syrian and Iraqi army leaders, for example, cannot use these qualities in the political arena, precisely because of their division. Sometimes these able men are left to the mercy of civilian and opportunistic groups within their midst. Lack of political leadership and cohesion among men reduces the usefulness of their military qualities. And, in matters of leadership, the civilian political organizations—Front Liberation Nationale, Muslim Brotherhood, Partie Populaire Syrienne, Ba'th —could teach the army. But these political groups are susceptible to the same conflicts as the New Middle Class, although the parties themselves may represent only sectors of that class.

Halpern's eulogy on Middle Eastern armies and their capability and potential cannot hold its own against the logic of theory or the burden of facts. The number of conditions under which the army may become the NMC[60] is reminiscent of Berger's propositions for Middle Eastern stable and powerful middle classes. The army as "the most powerful stratum of the new middle class" only existed in Nasser's Egypt after the military dictatorship between 1952 and 1956 had eliminated all political opposition. Halpern is not willing to forecast the next developments in the Arab world or in Egypt. But his concept implies a prediction which, in turn, threatens his basic assumptions. The existence of strong civilian members of the same strata in Syria does not demonstrate the so-called resiliency of the country. The rivalries between civilians and militarists, and within the military, demonstrate that when either group comes to power, it is not in fact "securely anchored." It shows, furthermore, that when the army is in power, it represents not the NMC but its ashes.

The danger for social scientists lies in trying to make a single theory account for too wide a variety of actual situations. The falls of Nkrumah, Ben-Bella and Sukarno demonstrate the need for comparative, dynamic explanation as a basis for social science theories. Casual explanations are valuable only where based on more durable theories than Halpern's; his concept of the NMC is weak, because it is based on a static explanation. "We speak of a static explanation," writes Harsanyi, "when a social variable is explained exclusively in terms of variables belonging to *the same time period.*"[61] Thus the potentials of the NMC, the intelligentsia, the army and all other "New Men" must be explained in terms of a dynamic model which "allow[s] for slow, delayed, or staggering adjustment, and which include[s] the social conditions of earlier periods (and/or the time trends due to the changes going on in society)."[62]

Political Mobilization and the Military

Is it possible for the revolutionary fervor expressed in the *Falsafat al-Qawmiyyah (The Philosophy of Nationalism)* and *Ikhtarna Lak (We Have Chosen for You)* propagandistic political literature to change Berger's "pliable" and "servile" bureaucrat[63] into an innovative and administrative political leader? Will the military succeed where the political parties have failed, in consolidating the new middle classes and leading them to sustained modernization and industrialization? Is the army really capable of marshalling mass support?

Consistent with the recent historical trend, Nasser and his followers have created bureaucracies to modernize Egypt. The Egyptian army officers, who are themselves products of the bureaucracy, prefer administrative to political solutions. They feel these are most suitable for modernization and for maintaining their authority; this preference is consistent with Egypt's history. Today, the dependent bureaucracies are run by the military in alliance with technological elites, and these groups take the place of the parties and independent associations essential for political growth and participation. Thus, voting in contemporary Egypt is not a political virtue, a conscientious act or mechanism of consensus. It is simply another etatist practice, since the army and its allies—among the new classes and within the salariat ask, not for actual political participation, but rather for plebiscitory approval of its integration into etatist politics.

The "Progressive Officer" model has failed to establish a successful land reform system, or to socially liberate the economically emancipated rural middle class, or the urban skilled workers. Neither the fellahin nor the unskilled urban workers have been given an equitable share in the economy. Above all, the economically liberated rural classes have had little or no share in politics. None of the economically liberated rural classes has become a part of the ruling elites. Only the officers, children of rural middle classes, have been given the chance for political mobility.

In the area of political mobilization, Nasser's political parties became instruments wed to institutionalize military praetorianism in Egypt. Political mobilization, even on a limited scale, collapsed along with the agrarian reforms. By 1971 the A.S.U., the party of mobilization, was in ruins, and political development—widening the scope and levels of political institutionalization[64]—has never taken place in Egypt.

4. POLITICAL POWER AND SOCIAL COHESION IN NASSER'S EGYPT

The thrust of the argument concerning a praetorian orientation is that protracted political institutionalization, a low level of social cohesion and the persistence of military rule all enhance praetorianism. In nonpraetorian states, the above conditions could initiate the movement toward praetorianism. Thus, in the next three chapters we will examine the relationship between political power and social classes in Egypt, the processes of political institutionalization of Nasser's Egypt; and the persistence of Nasserite praetorianism in Egypt.

The Two Elite Clusters of Egypt

The connection between Egypt's social classes and its political power is based on the country's power pyramid, with two ruling elites sharing the top, and the rural middle and skilled urban workers' classes distributed through the lower part.

The concept of elites has developed greatly since Mosca, Pareto, and Michels first formulated their theories at the turn of the century. More recently, Harold D. Lasswell's formulation stressed elite research on the empirical level.[1] However, a review by Dankwart Rustow[2] of the research done thus far reveals that recent quantitative and empirical studies of elites have not established a proper "correlation between political power and social status."[3] Therefore Rustow, supporting R. Bendix and S.M. Lipset's contention that the facts of politics must be studied in their own right and not merely inferred from the politician's social background, is critical of most recent empirical elite studies.[4]

Nasser's Egypt contains two clusters of elites, one acting as a ruling class, the other as a strategic elite primarily concerned with administration and technocracy.

The Ruling Elite

We can identify Egypt's top echelon of political power by using a modified definition of Pareto, Mosca and Michels's ruling class. The ruling class, thus modified, is not a natural aristocracy; it need not be associated exclusively with authoritarian or democratic regimes; and it could be located anywhere on the left-right continuum. A ruling class does not need to be cohesive, or politically effective, or restricted in size.

The stratocracy that dominated Nasser's Egypt was not merely another elite category among a variety of elites.[5] It was a ruling group because it has a "group identity derived from sources other than their political function."[6] Its scope of authority was relatively wide and diffuse,[7] and its sources of recruitment and internal organization differentiate it from the strategic elites in Egyptian society. It was the political leadership in power.[8] A ruling group could be distinguished by its long-term rule, its inaccessibility and its relatively small and concentrated size. Yet, it can also thrive in a transitional state.[9] It also restricts the formation of other political groups from which competing political elites could spring.

Nasser's elite was a ruling group not only because it was "suffused with strong sentiments of moral indignation and social protest,"[10] but also because its members had significant political authority. They are an example of the classical governing elite, although they lack the requirements of birth and wealth attached to the Pareto natural aristocracy. According to Ralf Dahrendorf, the Michels-Mosca-Pareto definition of an elite has serious weaknesses—at least in highly complex, democratic and industrial societies. I prefer to modify their definition for the praetorians": the politically governing elite." According to Dahrendorf, the Michels-Mosca-Pareto definition of an elite fails "to relate [conflict groups] to the crucial category of imperatively coordinated associations."[11] Thus, "ruling groups are . . . no more than ruling groups within defined associations. In theory, there can be as many competing, conflicting, or coexisting dominating conflict groups in a society as there are associations."[12] This elite definition prevents us from identifying the ruling class as the only political elite in circumstances where other associations exist, containing other defined ruling groups or elites within them. The first echelon of Egypt's political pyramid is the most influential political elite in that society; the echelons below consist of strategic elites, some with clearly defined and highly restricted political functions, others recruited only to participate in political decision making.

The political power of the ruling elite must also be measured by the existence or absence of organized political opposition. Thus, the absence of a mass political party and organized political associations in Egypt increases the political power of its ruling class.

The amount of political power the ruling group shares with other elites also determines its level of political power. In Nasser's Egypt, several measures have been adopted to decrease the power of competing political bureaucracies and their elites, in a conscious effort to promote Egypt's single political elite. Among these measures are: the diffusion of the officers' class into new bureaucracies; the use of the Arab Socialist Union as a clearinghouse for selecting "acceptable" candidates for the government bureaucracy; the cooperation of the old entrepreneurial and economic classes; the emulation of professional classes; the cautious land reform programs; and the higher proportions of key political offices in relation to the Civil Service. Sadat, on the other hand, uses the permanent purge to limit political competition. Sadat's regime is much more restrictive, and thus more praetorian, than Nasser's.

The ruling elite model has been unpopular among political and social scientists since the criticism of Robert Dahl and others.[13] According to these critics, the ruling elite model of the old Michels-Mosca-Pareto school is ambiguous; while the models of C. Wright Mills and Floyd Hunter are fallible and, at best, "interpret complex ruling elite formations, political systems essentially as instances of a ruling elite."[14] However, Dahl's critique only applies to complex political systems in highly industrial societies. So does C. Wright Mills' elite theory. Based on Mills' concept of institutional and corporate linkages i.e. the industrial military-multiversity complex, the theory is that the directorship-general of society or power elite is linked at the above institutional level. This elite theory also implies a conspiratorial aspiration on the part of the power elite, that is, the power elite is continuous, cohesive and possesses a common will for action to *politically* dominate society. In fact, the existence of a praetorian ruling class as the political elite demonstrates the transitional nature of Egypt's political system. This is further shown by the fact that Egypt's ruling class can be well defined and easily identified; that its preferences regularly prevail; and that it is not complex and linked via large-scale corporate institutions.[15] As James Heaphy demonstrates, the Egyptian decentralization of government is "nonpolitical" in character, and the absence of "uncertainty relationships" between the governors and the people demonstrates the former's political impotence and the latter's meager demand and political input.[16] Nasser's elite is certainly not the same as Mills' power elite.

Domination by a political ruling group or, in the case of Egypt, by a ruler type praetorian group is also an indication of advanced praetorianism. The restricted ruling political elite is a most useful criterion for the study of developing states in the presence of local polarity, low political institutionalization and inadequate distribution of political power. A ruling class need not be highly cohesive to be able to dominate under praetorian conditions. That group which has the most dominant political power will rule, regardless of its cohesiveness, although some form of cohesion is necessary to govern in a praetorian state.

In Egypt, from 1953-1970, at the top of the pyramid of political power stood the *Rais*, Gamal Abdel Nasser. He was the most important decision maker, wielding almost unlimited executive and legislative power. Aiding the Rais were former members of the Free Officers and of the Revolutionary Command Council, which had been abolished as an organization in 1956.[17] Officers, and particularly veteran Free Officers, held the highest positions in Nasser's cabinets until 1966.

Identification of the ruling elite begins with the study of Egypt's formal and effective political power structures, the government and the cabinet. Since Egyptian political parties and interest groups had been reduced to playing the role of governmental instruments, the real power holders were the senior members of Nasser's cabinets. During the eight Nasser cabinets, the percentage of officer members fluctuated from 45 percent in the 1952 cabinet, to 32 percent in the 1956 cabinet, to 47 percent in the 1965 cabinet.[18] The June 1967 disaster finally caused the ouster of Veteran Free Officers from Nasser's 1968 cabinet—although only one Shafi'i had ever held a political office.

Between 1952 and 1967, each of the four top governmental positions—President, First Vice-President, Prime Minister and Senior Vice-President—has been held by only one civilian.*[19] The army as a ruling group has been diffused into the crucial governmental (and Arab Socialist Union party) positions, in economics, industry and diplomacy. Be'eri estimates that this ruling group constituted 1,000 loyal officers, headed and directed by the small group of veteran Free Officers.[20] In the classic manner of the ruling group, it is replenished by the same group, in this case the army. Since 1952, no group has enjoyed a greater increase in its share of the highest political offices. The regime of Sadat is completely dependent on the military.

---

*Between 1967 and Nasser's death in 1970, the post of First Vice-President was abolished, and the *Rais* was the only civilian officeholder.

The most comprehensive analysis (although it uses a small sample) of the social origin and family background of Egyptian army officers has been conducted by Be'eri.[21] His analysis of 87 Egyptian officers killed in the Palestine War of Liberation from 1947-1949 (2.9 percent of the total officer class in 1948-1949) illustrates the conspicuous position of the rural middle class and its urban offshoots in the Egyptian Officers Corps, from which the Free Officers sprang.[22]

The similar social origins and family background of Free Officers, especially the senior members, could demonstrate the potential of the ruling elite to act as a cohesive class. However, this is not equivalent to a political class, although it could be a crucial factor in elite political formation and influence.

The close and clandestine nature of the ruling elite, as well as its members' common backgound, encourages common social action, but does not guarantee common political action or ideology. On the whole, Nasser's officer group has been a closed group which, despite its primary group bonds, was not cohesive politically. It could be argued that the Free Officers, having emerged from an identifiable stratum of the Egyptian army, having experienced the Palestine campaign together, and having endured the surveillance of Faruq's secret police, developed political cohesion and some form of common political action. But it was a short-lived era of political cohesion. Events after 1952 show that the rise of the Free Officers was less dependent on social origins than on common bonds connected with the army, as conspirators. Another weakness in the argument that the political power of the Egyptian officers came from their common social background is the fact that they acted as individuals, not as a class. Common descent, social class and economic interest have not been sufficient to make the Egyptian rural middle classes, and their urban offshoots, a ruling elite. The army elite did not become a ruling class and did not create at least some form of political cohesion because it had a common social class, family background and group identity. Nor did it so because of its clandestine nature, or the hostility of the senior officers of the old regime, or even the traumatic lessons of Palestine. Rather, the army elite became a ruling class through antagonism to the civilian politicians, and, above all, through the longevity of its rule and its independent control over political power, which has excluded all other elites in Egypt since 1952. The ruling elite now has a monopoly on political power since it has vanquished its antagonists old and new. Although Nasser purged many army officers from his government after 1967, the chances for the future return of the military to political power are better than ever, particularly as Egypt's army, under intensive training by the Soviets, prepared for the next round of the "Liberation of Palestine" in October 1973. Social origins and political cohesion do not explain the political behavior and elite formation of either Nasser's or Sadat's regime. Both are restrictive praetorian ruling classes—the former more secure and the latter precarious, but praetorian nonetheless.

The Strategic Elite

The second type of elite in Nasser's Egypt, the strategic elite, is distinguished by its members, consisting of "specialists in excellence."[23] It is an elite of merit, representing Egypt's professional and technocratic group. Yet some influential members of this elite have been accepted into the ruling class, because of the political recruitment means employed by Nasser's inner circle. The strategic elites were recruited on the basis of function, rather than group and kinship, as is the case with the ruling group. Because the Free Officers are the ruling group and many members of the strategic elite are recruited from, or co-opted by, the army, this type of recruitment helps diffuse the ruling group into all the key centers of political power. Thus, former army officers have certain privileges which other members of the strategic elite do not enjoy. For example, Free Officers among the strategic elite have ruling class advantages and enjoy specific types of political influence which their functional equivalents, the strategic elite, do not.

Among the strategic elites, the officers are assigned to coordinate governmental departments, to run industries and economic enterprises, to inculcate the "Egyptian Revolution" or Nasserite concept of politics into the bureaucracy, and to administer land reform. Although performing as an elite of merit, they also behave as a ruling class. In this case, the army, as a ruling class, and the reservoir from which this core group of the strategic elite is recruited, are the same.[24] This stratum of the strategic elites wields great political power, not because of its economic function, but because it is recruited from the ruling class. The military under Sadat clearly demonstrates this argument. Another stratum of the strategic elites, not recruited from the army, represents the technical, professional and economic groups and is composed of lawyers, physicians, engineers, university professors and former financiers and businessmen considered untainted by the "corruption" of the former regime. This technical-professional-economic elite, unlike the political elite of former Wafdists, journalists and politicians, does not represent a threat to the political elite. The members of this technical elite are mostly retained for their valuable skills, which could not be replaced by the ruling class or other elites of merit. Under Sadat this group has declined.

On the whole, since Sadat's coup of May 1971, officers have headed Egypt's political departments: the Defense Ministry, the Ministry of National Guidance and the Foreign Office. The nonruling elite of merit is spread throughout the functional and economic departments—the Ministries of Finance, Economics and Industry. The major circulation of elites under Sadat is between and within the military.

Even in the latter ministries, former army men had top positions, and the key governmental enterprises are still headed by former officers. This is true of the Suez Canal project, the Aswan High Dam and Desert Reclamation authorities, as well as the directorship of Bank Misr (the National Bank), and the directorship of the Nile Navigation Company. Thus, in the key economic and public enterprises, the managerial and financial elite of the previous regime is subordinated to the military officers.

The Foreign Office was dominated by the officers; Mahmud Riad was in charge of foreign affairs between 1967-1972, and has been in the Foreign Service since before 1952 (he was also a member of the Egyptian delegation to the Rhodes Egyptian-Israeli armistice in 1949). In 1952, 25 of the 58 Egyptian ambassadors were former officers; in 1964, 43 out of 73 were former officers.[25] The Secret Police is similarly staffed by the military, although its leaders—including several officers—were purged and tried during the 1968 Cairo military trials. With the purge of the army in 1967, the strategic elites were expected to gain a temporary ascendance, until the army regained its influence. Since the Sadat coup, the army has regained its influence. However, we do not yet know about any major changes in the strategic elite composition, except for the fact that more military men will be recruited.

The Free Officers soon found that the principles of the Egyptian Revolution were not promptly accepted by civil servants. Later, when the regime became more confident of the bureaucracy's loyalty, the problem of providing positions for the junior officers arose. This was solved by moving them into the foreign service. There they felt well rewarded, since the status of diplomats is high in Egypt, and because their tasks in the Foreign Service were less difficult than those available in the Ministries of Interior, Social Affairs, Agrarian Reform or Education.

To establish the fact that the military is the political ruling group in Egypt does not explain why this is so, or the consequences of its rule. Praetorian rule is elitist, narrow and concentrated. This military ruling group is small; its roots are in the rural middle classes; its education is not above the high school level (except courses in foreign military academies);[26] it is a closed group, acting as a caste; and it is secretive. An analysis of the military as a ruling political group should explain what type of political actions this elite prefers; to what extent it is committed to the public good and modernization; to what extent, in short, praetorian rule serves public welfare in Egypt.[27]

Answering some of the questions of what ruling elites do rather than what they are[28] requires an investigation of the social classes which benefitted from the Egyptian Revolution and a determination of whether the ruling class has established, in combination with these groups, a wider spectrum of political power.

The Rural Middle Class and the Urban Workers

In 1956, the leaders of the Egyptian Revolution proclaimed that, once the political revolution was achieved—ousting the imperialists, the political parties and the court—the social revolution would inevitably follow. This "social revolution" was meant to include social and land reform, and end feudalism and the remnants of social inequality in Egypt.

Two classes benefitted directly from Nasser's social revolution: the rural middle class and its urban offshoots, and the skilled working class.

The Rural Middle Class and the Revolution. The real beneficiaries of Nasser's two unsuccessful agrarian reforms, in 1952 and 1961, have been the owners of between 10 and 100 *feddans** of land. Tables 1 and 2 indicate six strata of land ownership. Three of them make up the rural middle class: the owners of 5-10, 10-50, and 50-100 feddans. Table 2 shows that, since the first agrarian reform of 1952, the average amount of land owned by those in the 5-10 feddans group had increased from 8.8 percent to 10.1 percent. In the second group, the owners of 10-50 feddans, the average land ownership decreased from 18.7 percent in 1952 to 14.9 percent in 1964; however, the amount of land this group possessed increased from 21.6 percent to 21.9 percent during the same period. Although the third group, the owners of 50-100 feddans, decreased from 71.5 percent to 65.3 percent in average ownership of land, the overall percentage of land owned by this group barely decreased—from 7.2 percent to 6.4 percent in that same period. In fact, this group profitted by the agrarian reform of 1952, for in 1961, it had owned a higher percentage of land (10.5 percent).

These figures indicate that the rural middle class was retained after the Revolution, and that in fact members of some strata in this class were able to improve their economic lot. The economic stability of this group, unharmed by agrarian reforms, is a highly significant

---

*A *feddan* equals 1.038 acres.

Table 1: DIVISION OF LANDED PROPERTY IN EGYPT, 1943-1964

Classification of Ownership (in feddans)	No. of Landowners (in thousands)				No. of feddans owned (in thousands)			
	1943	1952	1961	1964	1943	1952	1961	1964
0-5	2,376	2,642	2,870	2,965	1,944	2,122	2,660	3,353
5-10	85	79	79	78	570	526	530	614
10-50	62	69	69	90	1,204	1,291	1,300	1,342
50-100	7	6	11	6	459	429	630	392
100-200	3	3	3	4	438	437	450	421
200+	2	2	2	—	1,245	1,117	430	—
Totals	2,535	2,801	3,034	3,143	5,860	5,982	6,000	6,122

Source: Gabriel Baer, "New Data and Conclusions about the Effects of Egypt's Land Reform," *Hamizrah Hehadash (The New East)*, Jerusalem, Israel, 16, no. 2 (1966): 176-78.

Table 2: INDIVIDUAL AVERAGE OWNERSHIP OF LAND AND PERCENTAGE OF LAND OWNED
BY EACH GROUP, 1943-1964

Classification of Ownership (in feddans)	Average Ownership of Land by Each Landowner (% in feddans)				Percentage of Land Owned by Each Group			
	1943	1952	1961	1964	1943	1952	1961	1964
0-5	0.8	0.8	0.9	1.1	33.2	35.4	44.3	54.7
5-10	6.7	6.7	6.7	7.9	9.7	8.8	8.8	10.1
10-50	19.4	18.7	18.8	14.9	20.6	21.6	21.7	21.9
50-100	65.6	71.5	57.3	65.3	7.8	7.2	10.5	6.4
100-200	146.0	145.7	150.0	105.2	7.5	7.3	7.5	6.9
200+	622.5	558.5	215.0	—	21.2	18.7	7.2	—
Total	2.3	2.1	1.9	1.9	100.00	100.00	100.00	100.00

Source: Gabriel Baer, "New Data and Conclusions about the Effects of Egypt's Land Reform," *Hamizrah Hehadash (The New East)*, Jerusalem, Israel, 16, no. 2 (1966): 176.

political factor in Nasser's Egypt.

The percentage of Egyptians in the poor peasant group (owners of less than 5 feddans) increased from 35.4 percent to 54.7 percent between 1952 and 1964. Yet, during the same period, the average land ownership of this group only rose from 8.8 percent to 10.1 percent.

Nasser's agrarian reforms did not eliminate the rich peasant category of people owning 100 to 200 feddans. Members of this group possessed 7.3 percent of the total land in 1952, and had suffered a loss of only 0.4 percent by 1964; while their number increased from 3,000 to 4,000 (see Table 2). Baer points out that neither of Nasser's agrarian reforms made nonowners of land into owners, although some 900,000 feddans were distributed among a million small landowners possessing 0.8 percent to 1.1 percent feddans.[29] Essentially, agrarian reform benefitted the Egyptian rural middle classes,[30] enchancing their economic stability. The real victims of the agrarian reform were the owners of 200 feddans or more, whose land was taken away completely after the 1961 reform. The elimination of these feudal classes created a political and economic power vacuum in rural Egypt, which the rural middle classes filled.

While the rural middle class did not assume the role played by the former feudal lords and rich peasants, it did assume a significant role among Egypt's strategic elites. The economic perseverance of this class demonstrates how little the Egyptian countryside had been disturbed by Nasser's social revolution. But the political influence of the rural middle class is severely limited in comparison with that of the ruling group; it may actually be equal to or below that of the strategic elites. The rural middle class is not much more politically potent than it was prior to 1952. The fact that many army officers are still drawn from this class does not mean it is a source of political power; it simply indicates the social origin of much of the Egyptian military. The source of the ruling group's political power is not the rural middle class, but the army. The rural middle class merely serves as a supporting group. Here lies the confusion of many writers who identify the army with the rural middle class and therefore consider that class a major source of political power in Egypt.

If we accept Leonard Binder's statement that the Preparatory Committee of 1961, which selected and nominated candidates for the Congress of Popular Forces in 1962, "provides a fairly good picture of the kind of people who run the Egyptian polity,"[31] then the rural middle class only represents 8 percent.[32] Some analysts argue that the rural middle class is better represented than this percentage indicates, because many village notables (*'umdah*) have relatives among both the ruling elite[33] and the strategic elites. But this still does not mean that the rural middle class is the source of political power in Egypt. That argument confuses a social elite with a ruling class. Suzanne Keller says:

> Most discussion of . . . ruling classes and elites fails to distinguish between two dimensions: the processes leading to the development of a core group . . . and the reservoir from which this core group is recruited.[34]

Such a confusion of political function and group identity leads to an exaggerated picture of the political role of the rural middle class in Egypt.

The Skilled Urban Workers. O'Brien claims that "those who have clearly and tangibly gained from the Egyptian Revolution are industrial workers and the beneficiaries of land reform."[35] Although the skilled workers were not politically mobilized in the 1950s, great changes occurred in the 1960s, with the rapid nationalization and heavy investment in industry. Their numerical increase is shown in Table 3.

The numbers for 1952-1961 are based on the yearly censuses in enterprises employing more than ten workers. After 1962, they are based on quarterly accounts and are only listed for industries employing more than 50 workers.

The addition of a force of 100,000 workers between 1950 and 1963 accounts for the end of the stagnation of the 1950s. According to Charles Issawi, workers in modern industry comprise a little more than 3 percent of the total Egyptian population and 10 percent of its urban population; the unskilled, domestic servants, handicrafts workers and the *lumpenproletariat* comprise 56 percent of the urban proletariat and 16.6 percent of the total population.[36] Significantly, the 3 percent of the population represented by Egypt's skilled workers have improved both their economic conditions and their political representation.

The rise of Egypt's skilled working class is also reflected in the governmental structures—in the Socialist Union, the

Table 3: NUMBER OF SKILLED WORKERS IN
EGYPTIAN POPULATION FROM 17,000,000 (1952)
TO 31,000,000 (1971)

Year	Workers
1952	272,156
1959	293,434
1961	399,998
1962	352,188
1963	384,490
1971	500,000*

*estimated

Source: *National Bank of Egypt Economic Bulletin,* No. 1 (1964), p. 115. Quoted in Avraham Ben Tsur, *Arab Socialism* (Tel Aviv: Kibbutz Movement Press, 1966).

Parliament and the Congress of Popular Forces. The representatives of this group held 13.5 percent of the seats in the 1964 Parliament.[37] The trade unions played a key role in Nasser's rise to power between 1952 and 1954. In fact, they were one of the few organized groups supporting him at that time; they helped him topple Nagib's "old parties" government coalition in 1954. Later, to control the potential power of labor and especially that of the skilled groups, Nasser recruited workers into government-controlled unions,[38] and banned strikes.

Along with the rural middle class, the skilled workers have improved their economic lot; but they have not increased their political power at the same rate, because representation in Nasser's Parliament does not constitute political power. The working class had a proportionally higher representation in the 1961 Preparatory Committee (11.2 percent) than did the rural middle class (8 percent).[39] The reason for the higher figure is that many so-called "workers" (officials of the Arab Socialist Union and of trade unions) actually belonged to the professional and governmental employee groups[40]—a stratum of the strategic elite.

The United Arab Republic's official division of political groups follows an occupational classification which distorts class origin and exaggerates the political power of those social classes that benefitted economically from the Egyptian Revolution. In the absence of categories based on criteria other than occupation, it is impossible to assess the political power of the various social and economic groups. Political power in Egypt depends on the Officer Corps as a ruling clique and on the strategic elites, both of which draw heavily on the upper strata of the rural middle class and on the skilled workers. However, neither Egypt's rural middle class nor its skilled working class serves as a major source of the country's political power.

The relationship between the rural middle classes and the army needs clarification. In some underdeveloped countries, the politically influential classes are closely related to the powerful economic groups. This was the case in Egypt before 1952, when senior positions in the bureaucracy, in the army and in the civil service were allocated to the ruling class—then a combination of the landed aristocracy, urban upper bourgeoisie and rich professionals. Members of the rural middle class only occupied those positions in the army and in the bureaucracy that corresponded to their own more modest political power. Thus a direct relationship existed between core political elites and the reservoir from which they came. Since 1952, however, the sons of the rural middle class (especially its two upper strata—owners of 10-50 and 50-100 feddans) should have become the ruling political elite. But, contrary to many people's expectations, this did not increase the political power of the rural middle classes. The army, having developed into the effective equivalent of a class, became the instrument of political power. Individuals were recruited to the ruling elite through the army, rather than through the rural middle class, whose political power had remained the same even though the Revolution's economic reforms had improved its economic lot. These conclusions reiterate my thesis on praetorianism: that military rule is politically restrictive and fails to integrate new men and economically and socially liberated groups and classes; that the level of political institutionalization is restricted, rigid and nonadaptive; that economic changes do not affect social cohesion on the distribution of political power; and that, above all, praetorian rule enhances the political power of the military and a persistent praetorian enhances praetorianism which, after a certain period of time, develops a momentum of its own. Furthermore, the utility of military rule is maximized under the ruler type of praetorianism, the type which has ruled Egypt for close to a quarter century.

The UAR government officially represented all of Egypt's political and societal functions—government, party, class interests—and skills, but it by no means includes all the various social and political groups. Rather, the UAR government avoided these differences, by simply denying their existence. The elite's base had been broadened by the dominance of the senior army officers, the former Free Officers and the better salaried professionals in the government bureaucracy. The government was still tightly controlled by former Free Officers and their bureaucratic-technocratic allies. The absence of political institutions or structures in Nasser's Egypt representing class and political cleavages does not mean that class, interest, social, political or ideological conflicts had disappeared. Rather, dissension resulting from decisions made at the top of the power pyramid had been silenced.

To sum up, Nasser's agrarian reforms were only partially successful. Although the power of the big landlords was curtailed, the landless and the owners of less than 1 feddan did not benefit from the reforms.[41] The rural middle class and even the rich peasants (owning 100-200 feddans) have benefitted economically from the agrarian reforms. During the period 1966-1967, a third agrarian reform, designed to restrict the power and wealth of people owning 20 feddans or more, was suggested in the Egyptian press,[42] indicating increased pressure on the regime to effect revolutionary change in the countryside. However, since the Six Days War of 1967, agrarian reform has been abandoned; thus, no third reform took place.

The 'umdah, the second stratum of the rural middle class, who owned 50 feddans or more before the Revolution and now own 10-20 feddans, have been sustained in powerful positions on the local level through Nasser's agrarian reforms. O'Brien observes that the Revolution has made little difference to the mass of Egypt's poor peasants, agricultural laborers and employees of noncorporate enterprises.[43]

The 1952 Nasser coup was planned, organized and executed entirely by the army, strictly for its own benefit, and with little or no support from other movements or classes, although the officers were inspired by a variety of nationalist, religious fundamentalist, fascist and anti-foreign groups. The 1958 Qassem coup in Iraq was also conceived, planned, organized and executed exclusively by the military, with no outside support. Iraq's military coup makers were supported by the United National Front (the bloc of anti-Hashemite, anti-monarchist parties), but the latter's help was not crucial for the coup's success.[44] In Syria, likewise, we know of no coup that was conceived, organized or executed by other class than the military, even if several coups were encouraged by the Ba'th party. The three successful coups in 1949 were planned by the army's high command, as was Adib Shishakly's coup in 1954. The 1961 coup against the UAR was conceived, planned and executed by the army as were the coups of 1963, 1966 and 1969. In none of these countries did the military represent the interests of the middle class (either old or "new"), or of any other class. Military rule in the Middle East indicates the chaos of social structure and the decadence of politics, two of the most significant characteristics of praetorianism.

Nasser's ruling elite apparently sought a formula for modernization and restricted political mobilization. It sought to sustain power without dealing with the problems of alienation and cleavages. This group was seeking to avoid the penalties of functional differentiation, without fragmenting Egypt's social order, or, for that matter, without encouraging pluralist community and political tendencies.[45]

The removal of foreigners and imperialist powers, the

political and economic elites of colonial Egypt, left a vacuum into which the army moved, as the new ruling group. Members of the native Egyptian ruling group, the court and the aristocracy, which also depended on foreign rule and finance, were expropriated, although some cooperated with the new army regime. The rural and urban middle classes, the small working classes and the urban intelligentsia work at cross purposes; thus their rivalry only furthers the army's position as the political elite of Egypt.

Such conditions prompted Nasser and the Free Officers to turn the army into a reservoir of political power, at the expense of the strategic and other elites, and at the price of restricting political mobilization of any group besides the rural middle classes and the urban industrial workers.

The regime's policy of restricted recruitment is intended to help it control change. Huntington argues that "the strength of political organizations and procedures varies with their *scope of support* and their level of institutionalization."[46] The military junta prefers a limited and highly restricted scope of support: from the military itself, the bureaucracy, the skilled workers and the rural middle classes. This formula of restricted and controlled political participation is not unique to Egypt; it has also been adopted by several other developing regimes, among them Indonesia and Pakistan.[47] The restriction of political participation is often related to sustained institutionalization, because the wider and more permanent the popular support, the more durable the political institutions.

Slowing down political mobilization can be a strategy of institutional development. Huntington suggests three methods of harnessing political mobilization: to increase the complexity of social structures; to limit or reduce communication in the society; and to minimize competition among various segments of the political elite.[48] Only the third measure has been used in Egypt. The failure of a concomitant growth in the complexity of social structures and of their political autonomy, and the continuous creation of false expectations of a wider political participation for new social groups while the power pyramid remains essentially unchanged, makes the motives of Nasser's followers in restricting political mobilization seem suspect. The restriction of political participation may be interpreted as a desire on the part of the military junta and its rural and urban allies to perpetuate themselves in power. This can be deduced, not from the failures of the regime, but from its achievements. Either Nasser failed to meet the participation crisis with a concentrated effort at recruiting political support, or the curtailment of participation was simply another measure for keeping the praetorian elite in power.

5. EXPERIMENTS IN PRAETORIANISM: NASSER'S REGIMES AND POLITICAL PARTIES

The major characteristic of a praetorian state is its low level of political institutionalization and support. Professor Huntington and I agree[1] that stable political parties with a wide scope of support and a high level of institutionalization are *necessary* conditions for a non praetorian system. Thus it becomes crucial to examine the efforts of Nasser and his successor in forming political parties. The stabilization and institutionalization of political parties are the major indicators of both the persistence (if it fails) and the disappearance (if it succeeds) of praetorianism.

Nasser governed Egypt from April 1954 until his death in November 1970. He came to power without institutionalized political legitimacy, but with experience and a profound political understanding of Egypt.

We have already analyzed the ideological foundation of Egyptian nationalism, as well as the processes of coup preparing and coup making. We have also examined Nasser's anti-political stance, and his idea for a political organization replacing the community solidarity structure that is absent from Egyptian society. Nasser was not a political philosopher, but as a pragmatist he made a considerable contribution to the new style of politics that has become prevalent in the Arab and sub-Saharan African worlds.

Before examining the dynamics of Nasser's political parties, let us turn first to a discussion of the evolution of praetorian regimes in the Middle East in general, and then to the specific evolution of Nasser's single party system.

The Structural Evolution of Military Praetorian Regimes

We have distinguished two basic types of praetorian armies, the arbitrator type and the ruler type. The major differences between them are the time limits they place on their own rule, and their orientations toward controlling the nation's executive. While the arbitrator type army imposes a fixed time limit on military rule and arranges to hand over the government to an "acceptable" civilian regime, the ruler type army believes in prolonged, even permanent, rule. The arbitrator type army, although it does not necessarily relinquish political influence, does believe in returning to the barracks on the condition that the army continue to act as a guardian of civilian authority and political stability. This was the essence of the Kemalist legacy in Turkey; the army serves as guardian of the constitution, from the barracks. The ruler type army not only does not set a time limit on military rule; it actually plans to establish itself as the legitimate political ruling group. First, it invents or adopts an ideological stance. Then it creates a political party within the army, a sort of executive committee made up of "free officers." The most significant contribution of Arab army officers to political control of executive power is the Revolutionary Command Council (RCC), an ad hoc military cabinet which runs the government and directs the society. The RCC is also in charge of eliminating opposition within the military and the society. It is the command post of military executive control. This type of instrument has been adopted in all praetorian Arab countries, and is gaining wide recognition in the sub-Saharan African nations dominated by the military. The ruler type of army has prevailed in all praetorian Arab countries—Egypt, Syria, Iraq, Libya, the Sudan. The ruler type praetorian army belongs to the second political generation, since its rise to power is based on its opposition to the "political corruption" of traditional parliamentary regimes, thus encouraging the development of authoritarian non-party or one-party systems. This does not mean that the officers are revolutionary; their sometimes self-proclaimed conversion to revolutionary causes is likely to be much more superficial than their anticonservatism. In fact, of all reformist groups in the praetorian state, the army tends to be the least reformist.

The evolution of executive control in both arbitrator and ruler type praetorianism follows a cyclical pattern, beginning with executive arbitration, developing into executive control, and then turning back to a type of arbitration. The institutional and structural arrangements of each praetorian regime type differ, according to its orientation. Both the arbitrator and the ruler type regimes develop political and structural arrangements appropriate to their roles. The syndrome, however, is more complex. Only the first wave of either type is close to the model; the second round of an arbitrator or ruler type becomes more

Figure 1: MODEL A*
THE ARBITRATOR REGIME TYPE

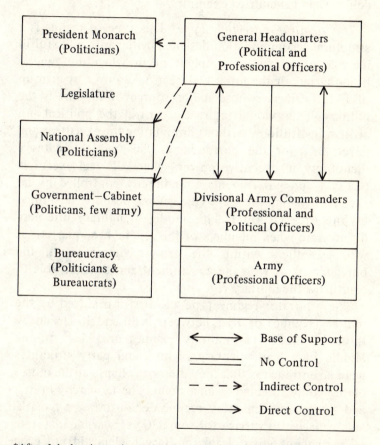

Head of State

| President Monarch (Politicians) | General Headquarters (Political and Professional Officers) |

Legislature

National Assembly (Politicians)

Government—Cabinet (Politicans, few army)

Divisional Army Commanders (Professional and Political Officers)

Bureaucracy (Politicians & Bureaucrats)

Army (Professional Officers)

←——→ Base of Support
═════ No Control
– – – ➢ Indirect Control
——➤ Direct Control

*After I had written about the above model and had designed my charts (models A, B, C) I came across Meir Pa'il's essay, "Patterns of Revolutionary Officers' Regimes in Iraq and Syria" *(Hamizrah Hehadash,* 1969, pp. 181-207) which inspired me to modify my charts following his designs. I am most grateful to Pa'il's ideas and to our long conversations on the above during the summer of 1970.

complex, even if the basic principles of the model remain correct. Here we will deal only with the ideal types of executive control—arbitrator and ruler—suggesting a number of case studies to explain the models, and using deliberately generalized examples.

The Arbitrator Regime Type. This type of regime is a structural accommodation designed by the military to fulfill its role of arbitrator. It might occur when the general headquarters of the army had been taken over by a group of Free Officers, whose major source of support is the military. They would indirectly control the political and civilian institutions, without dominating the executive, the government or the bureaucracy. This model creates a dichotomy in executive power, where the real executive (cabinet and government) is indirectly controlled by an executive behind the scene (the general headquarters, ruled by the Free Officers). This model of military rule may disintegrate when members of the general headquarters, as well as others within the army, combine with the bureaucracy or with the government and thus are able to overthrow the military regime.

The arbitrator regime type was first introduced by the military regimes of Iraq between 1936 and 1941 and by three of the Syrian military regimes in 1949.[2] In the Middle East, parliamentary regimes and party structures were so entrenched that they did not collapse at the outset of the coups directed against them. The monarchy in Iraq and Syria's parliamentary regime demonstrated a remarkable capacity to survive for some 30 years, while in a state of permanent crisis. Iraq's military leaders did not even contemplate overthrowing the monarchy until 1958, nor did the Syrian army seriously consider arresting parliamentary government before 1966. In fact, the Ba'th party, Syria's sponsor of military interventionism, advocated sustaining parliamentary and party rule at least until 1966.

Middle Eastern military leaders have generally found the arbitrator regime model unsatisfactory, for two major reasons. Indirect rule over the executive does not permit the military to completely control the failures or antagonisms that occur within the government and the bureaucracy, and between these and the military. Second, because of their semiindependent rule, political parties, civilian institutions and the bureaucracy can successfully challenge the military leaders. Ironically, the arbitrator type regime, which was designed to strengthen political authority and create order in the Middle East, actually helped strengthen the radical, nationalist groups and parties, while it weakened military authority.

The short-lived coalition of the arbitrator regime, between progressives, politicians, ideologues and the professional military, usually evolves into a military dictatorship which ousts all civilians from executive power and establishes an army executive arm such as the ALM (Arab Liberation Movement) in Syria, between 1952 and 1953, and the RCC in Egypt and other Arab military regimes, since 1953.

The Ruler Regime Type. The ruler type of regime, represented in the graph as Model B, is a modification of Model A (the arbitrator regime), designed to overcome the latter's failures. Here we find the perfect domination of the military over the executive, as the Revolutionary Command Council is established as the instrument for controlling the executive. In this ruler type of praetorianism, the head of the RCC is also both president and prime minister of the country, while the major source of support is still the general headquarters of the army. In this model, however, the RCC is composed entirely of nonpolitical officers, to avoid any chance of a coalition between the politicians and the military-bureaucratic alliance. The head of the RCC can sometimes relinquish his position as president to a civilian, but only under the condition that direct military rule over the bureaucracy will continue. There is a good chance that the legislature will be abolished, or else be completely dominated by the military. Once this type of regime becomes fully established, as we shall see in the graph of Model C, it will pack the

Figure 2: MODEL B
THE RULER REGIME TYPE

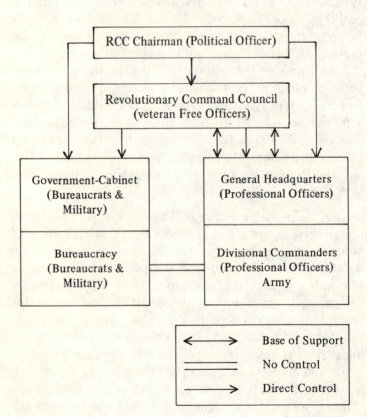

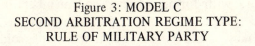

Figure 3: MODEL C
SECOND ARBITRATION REGIME TYPE:
RULE OF MILITARY PARTY

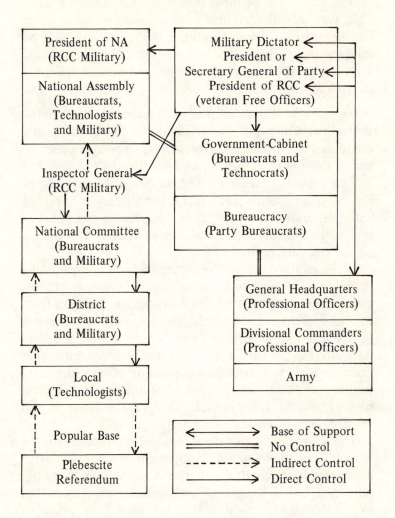

President of NA (RCC Military)

National Assembly (Bureaucrats, Technologists and Military)

Inspector General (RCC Military)

National Committee (Bureaucrats and Military)

District (Bureaucrats and Military)

Local (Technologists)

Popular Base

Plebescite Referendum

Military Dictator
President or
Secretary General of Party
President of RCC
(veteran Free Officers)

Government-Cabinet (Bureaucrats and Technocrats)

Bureaucracy (Party Bureaucrats)

General Headquarters (Professional Officers)

Divisional Commanders (Professional Officers)

Army

←————————→ Base of Support
════════════ No Control
- - - - - - -> Indirect Control
————————→ Direct Control

legislature with former officers and members of its own political party. Thus the cabinet-government and the bureaucracy both become a mixture of soldiers and bureaucrats, both of them firmly controlled by the RCC. This type of ruler regime first appeared in Syria under Colonel Adib Shishakly, who in 1952 transformed the military regime from Model A to Model C by uniting the army's general headquarters and the government under the control of a Revolutionary Command Council.

Back to the Arbitrator Regime. In the case of Model C, the military dictator, the head of the RCC, still totally dominates the executive. His major source of support remains the military high command. The RCC head then appoints loyal professional and patrimonial-oriented officers to general headquarters; and the military is rewarded with corporate autonomy. Thus, the relationship between the military dictator and the high command is both corporate and patrimonial.

If the military dictator is successful both in establishing order and in respecting the military's corporate orientation, the army returns to the barracks and switches from the ruler to the arbitrator role. The praetorian cycle is now complete: from abritrator to ruler type regime, and then back to the arbitrator type. If the military intervenes again, it may face both the opposition of the successful military dictator turned head of state, and the political organization at his disposal. Thus, the military is still divided, even though it is back in the barracks.

The second source of direct control and support for the Model C regime is a political movement or a political party dominated by the RCC. In the Arab Middle East, the military either initiates such political movements, or takes over established radical nationalist parties, in order to legitimize its own rule.

The Evolution and Dynamics
of Nasser's Political Parties

Before we discuss the specific political structures established by Nasser, it may be useful to explore Nasser's aversion to party politics structures. A   radical nationalist, Nasser felt that the government should not be tampered with. "We should be entirely irresponsible," he said, "if we allowed our enemies to tamper with the government machinery."[3] He considered government machinery to be the responsibility of the "internal" Egyptian group of Nasser and his cohorts. Political parties, in Nasser's view, are tools of capitalistic democracy, of bankers and pashas; they are partisan instruments of the feudal classes. "The dictatorship from which we have suffered under the name of democracy," says Nasser, "was the dictatorship of capital, feudalism under the name parliament." Nasser continues:

> Political democracy cannot be a reality unless there is social justice and social democracy and unless there are equal opportunity between the capitalist and the worker and between the feudalist and the agricultural laborer. One has plenty of money and can have a good dinner and one has no money to pay for dinner. Capitalists and feudalists want to hold general elections according to Western methods adopted by capitalist countries in which the minority enjoys all the influence and has an abundance of money. The political parties serve the interests of feudalists and capitalists.[4]

The function of the RCC was to establish political influence over the Nasser group. Nasser was aware that the Officers Corps were on the whole not political,* that the

---

*The number of politically active officers in the Egyptian army before 1952 was never over 300, with less than 50 officers who were real activists, out of an Officer Corps of some 20,000 members.[5]

few who were politically oriented were also isolated and divided; and that most of the politically oriented officers were merely the political agents of radical and social parties and movements heading the military cells of their respective groups. Nasser established the FOC (Free Officer Corps) to provide these politically oriented officers with an autonomous political organization. The FOC was an executive committe made up of 11 members: Nasser, Sadat, Zakariyah and Khaled Muhi al-Din, Abdel-Hakim 'Amer, Gamal and Salah Salem, Tawrat 'Ukasha, al-Mun'im a-Ra'uf, Hasan Ibrahim and Latif al-Baghdadi. Three of these men—Nasser, 'Amer and Zakariyah Muhi a-Din— acted as the core group.[6] The FOC established a miniature political organization with five departments: Manpower, Terrorism, Propaganda, Finance and Welfare. The first political act credited to FOC was the defeat of Faruq's candidate for the presidency of the Officers Corps.[7] They also organized guerrilla action against the British in the Suez.

The FOC served another purpose as well—loyalty screening. Nasser would periodically meet with the group in seminar fashion, to discuss Egyptian history and politics. Thus he was able to do the screening personally, while observing the viewpoints, character, behavior and expectations of the participants.[8] Thus, these "seminars" were designed to encourage group cohesion and to distinguish friend from foe, dependable from frivolous candidates for FOC membership and action. Hence the FOC was the first officer's consolidated-kinship group in the history of modern Arab military intervention.†

---

†'Abd al-Qasim of Iraq (1958-1963) and the "Alawi group of Asad-Jadid (February 1966-1970) succeeded in emulating the FOC. But Shishakly's Arab Liberation Movement of 1952 failed to serve the same purpose and he was unable to sustain his military dictatorship.

The need for an executive committee of the FOC immediately became apparent. The struggle for power against Nagib, the Wafd and above all the Muslim Brotherhood[9] and dissident officers called for an executive body to plan, consolidate and operationalize the July coup. The Revolutionary Command Council originated as part of the FOC group in 1949 and became an autonomous and cohesive cabal in the regime of Nagib between July 1952 and April 1954. The RCC was the political instrument which established the Nasser group in power in April 1954. Between 1952-1954, the RCC was also established to recruit support for the FOC and Nasser, and to abolish the University Students' Union—with the help of the radical MBs (Muslim Brotherhood Members). The RCC, under Nasser's supervision, had already demonstrated the pattern of Nasserite rule: clandestine, quiescent manipulation of competing rivals (Wafdist, MB and assorted FOC officers), the end product of which was Nasser's personal dictorship over Egypt, via the RCC.

The RCC as an executive committee for the Liberation Rally since 1953 functioned not unlike the FOC, as the sole representative of the military coup makers. Nasser himself participated in its design and worked closely on the organizational details of the Liberation Rally-RCC.[10] The major functions of the RCC were to eliminate opposition parties and personalities, to organize the masses, and to establish a political organ for Nasserite legitimacy and support.[11] The basic structure of the Liberation Rally was patterned after that of the RCC. Its President, General Nagib, was intended to be a figurehead. The Secretary General, the all-powerful man dominating policy and appointments, was Gamal Abdel Nasser. There were also Deputy Secretary General and an Inspector General: the Deputy was the operating arm of Liberation Rally, and the Inspector General was in charge of

Liberation Rally's political cells and local organs.[12] The Central Executive Committee of the Liberation Rally was composed of the same personnel as the RCC, to insure FOC ideology and domination over the central bodies of the Liberation Rally. The RCC was successful in dominating the Liberation Rally, and in duplicating the functions of Liberation Rally's Central Executive Committee. Nasser preferred a political organization such as the Liberation Rally, as an organ for rule and for "revolutionary" activities. Basically, Nasser opted for the formation of a mass party with extremely limited, political functions. In fact, Nasser's concept of the Liberation Rally mobilizing and "revolutionizing" Egypt was necessitated by the political needs of the military dictatorship at the time. Not until the collapse of the UAR in 1961 would Nasser modify this concept of party organization and function.

The Liberation Rally proved a failure as a mass organization, and it also failed to achieve the popularity of its major rival, the Muslim Brotherhood, the only legal party between 1952 and 1954. The Liberation Rally proved incapable of recruiting a leadership group to operationalize its goals. Thus the Egypt Nasser inherited was politically divided, fratricidally torn and socially fragmented. The Liberation Rally did not become a link between the center and the periphery, as intended. In fact, the Liberation Rally, designed as a participating party, proved a virtually total failure. Now the RCC had to make changes in its structure, in order to assume the responsibility for the Liberation Rally's functions. Having failed to gain mass support, Nasser now opted for widening the scope of the RCC and of his personal role and office. Between 1953 and 1955, the RCC was purged of its "ideologues" on both the left and the right.[13] Several new members joined the RCC: including members of the "second generation" Free Officers, the formerly nonpolitical officers and new recruits. The growth of the RCC was parallel to the percentage of officers in the cabinet, which declined from 45 percent in April 1954, to 32 percent in September 1956.[14] The military establishment and especially the army's high command were also purged of RCC's political opposition; and new professional nonpolitical senior officers (several of them from pre-1952 groups) were elevated to the high command. Divisional commanders were clearly nonpolitical, professional soldiers. This new composition weakened the RCC and strengthened the power of the *Rais*. A special office, that of president, was established in 1956, thus elevating Nasser above the RCC. The president reserved sole power in appointment and dismissal of the prime minister, the cabinet, the commander-in-chief of the army, and the senior officers. Supporting power was still derived from the army, but was not entirely dependent on senior officers. Civil servants were also recruited to the RCC, thus further weakening the influence of the military and the FOC veterans, and therefore that of the RCC. At least until 1961, the military remained the major source for recruitment to RCC, the cabinet, the government and the bureaucracy. Thus, prior to 1961, the military provided Egypt with most of its political, bureaucratic and industrial elites. To strengthen his personal power and weaken the RCC, Nasser then established a new political participatory structure, the National Union.

The National Union and the Socialist Union: Two Nasserite Anti-Political Experiments

On June 19, 1956, Premier Nasser proclaimed the end of martial law, an act symbolic of the consolidation of the

Free Officers' power. With the opposition crushed, Nasser and his group were ready to enforce the project for Egypt's future formulated in the constitution which had been presented to the country earlier that year. On June 23, the voters approved the constitution by plebiscite, and elected Gamal Abdel Nasser president. As the only candidate, he received all but 2,857 of the 5,508,291 votes cast; of 5,498,271 total people voting on the issue, only 10,046 voted against the constitution. Three new ministries, reflecting the regime's new social and economic objectives and managerial orientations, were set up: Industry (under 'Aziz Sidqi, an engineer); Agrarian Reform (under Sayyid Mar'i, an agricultural engineer); and Communications (under Mustafa Khalil Kamal, a railroad engineer).[15]

At the same time, three former members of the RCC and of the Liberation Rally cabinet moved to noncabinet positions: Gamal Salem to head governmental organization and the Civil Service; Hasan Ibrahim to become Director of the National Planning Council; and Anwar al-Sadat, one of Nasser's closest associates, to act as Secretary General of the Islamic Congress. The placement of Nasser's trusted associates in these positions indicated the increased importance of the tasks the holders of these offices were to perform, and the emergence of a new attitude toward public policy.

The constitution also provided for the establishment of a political organization. Chapter Six ("Transitional and Final Provisions"), Article 192 reads: "The people of Egypt shall form a National Union *[Ittihad Qaumi]* to accomplish the aims of the Revolution and to encourage all means to give the nation a solid foundation in the political, social, and economic realms."[16] The formal decree creating this party was issued in mid-1957, and the National Union participated in the elections in the summer of that same year. Anwar al-Sadat was appointed its Secretary General.

During 1958, Sadat published the National Union's principles and aims, first in a series of articles which appeared in the daily *al-Gumhuriyyah* (The Republic) and then in a pamphlet, *Qa'idah Sha'biyyah* (The Popular Base).[17] It had been apparent since the 1952 coup, he argued, that the RCC lacked the "necessary link" with the people. The National Union was now to supply this link, with a new political unit called *Qa'idah Sha'biyyah*. The National Union was meant to be a popular instrument, a party of solidarity. It was not supposed to be either a governmental organ—although, in fact, it became one—or a representative party, since it did not recognize classes, groups, or competing ideologies. Al-Sadat states that:

> The National Union is not a party or an abstract idea; it is a way of protecting the spirit and there is no other way. It is not an expedient freely adopted, but a necessity forced upon us, dictated by our new conditions and our new responsibilities.[18]

Nasser also announced the aims of the National Union, both at home, to establish a democratic social welfare society; and abroad, to achieve independence and freedom for Arabs, and to pursue Arab unity under Egyptian auspices.

The international objectives of the National Union were embodied in the union with Syria, announced on February 1, 1958, and constitutionally effected on March 5, 1959. This emphasis on Egypt's "Arabness" was not limited to discussions about the National Union. The 1956 Constitution itself had proclaimed Egypt "a sovereign independent Arab state," and "the Egyptian people [were] described as an integral part of the Arab nation."[19] It is doubtful that a union of the type attempted with Syria was specifically intended at the time the constitution was written; nor was it an original goal of the National Union. Rather, Egypt's intentions at that time were international only in the sense that it wanted a united Arab foreign policy, with Egypt setting the pace.

It was the Syrian Ba'th party, rather than Nasser, which wanted the union in the form it took. The Ba'th thought it could strengthen itself through the union, but Nasser wanted the Ba'th dismantled, with the National Union acting to unify the two countries. In fact, any discussion of the United Arab Republic is impossible without a simultaneous discussion of the National Union. But before examining the extension of the National Union to Syria or its actual organization, further discussion of its ideology and proposed objectives is necessary.

The Ideology of the National Union

The National Union was intended to accomplish the Triple Revolution, as stated by Nasser in his speech before the National Union Congress of July 9, 1960. The first of these was the "national" revolution of all Arab countries struggling against colonialism.

The second [was] the Arab revolution which urges its nationals to pass the artificial barriers and knock down the hurdles that represent false frontiers invented by invaders who spread dissension and suspicion. And the third, the social revolution which calls for an honourable living for every member of Arab society in fulfillment of social equality which is the mainstay of every national structure.[20]

Thus Nasser still felt that the Arab countries were threatened by the imperialists, who fomented divisions in the Arab world. Consequently, *Al-Isti'mar* (imperialism) was the chief national villain for all Arabs who subscribed to National Union principles. To combat imperialism and its instruments of divisiveness, such as competing political parties, Arabs were obliged to unite. However, this process of unification was specifically intended to be led by Egypt, for as the creator of the National Union, Egypt took upon herself the responsibility of defending the Arab world against the imperialists.[21]

In effect, the accomplishment of these goals—i.e., the national and anti-imperial revolutions—would have meant Egyptian hegemony in the Arab world. In the case of union with Syria, the actual result was domination by Egypt. Since the National Union was to be the instrument of unification, and since parties were considered divisive instruments, Nasser attempted to eliminate the Syrian parties, especially the Ba'th and the Communists.

The specific diplomatic and international power gains that Egypt was attempting to obtain by taking up the banner of Arab unity, were, of course, played down in official speeches. And as Egypt's actions became increasingly and more obviously self-aggrandizing, the official line more stridently proclaimed the ideal goals, with special emphasis on the ever present threat of imperialism. The foreign devil theory was used more and more often in Syria, as the failure of the unification scheme became more and more apparent.[22]

In the third revolution, the social one, two basic themes can be identified: the theme of social democracy and economic equality, and the theme of the uniqueness of the Arab world, which requires special solutions for its problems.

Nasser, speaking on the theme of social democracy on the ninth anniversary of the July coup, said:

> We should establish a new democracy and a new state with new political, economic and social systems. We must prove that our

socialism means the Liberation of man [sic] from bondage in all its forms. The socialism we are working for means both social and political democracy. We must build a new state in all its aspects, to be based on justice and equal opportunities.[23]

This new state was to be built through national planning and by the rational allocation of resources, so that the fruits of the people's labor would be used for the general good of the people, and not for the benefit of a small group of persons. The responsibility for the just distribution of rewards was to be placed on the officials of the state; but there was relatively little emphasis on the mobilization of the people, so that they could effectively observe and control the officials' conduct. Along with this emphasis on management and planning, Nasser attacked the remnants of feudalism as well as capitalist practices, claiming that both worked to the advantage of the few by using the labor of many. Nasser and his propagandists emphasized that, without the initial creation of social democracy, political democracy would not be possible.

Egyptian and Arab social democracy, its proponents claimed, must be different from European socialism. This difference was defined by Kamal Rifa't (ideologue of the Arab Socialist Union until 1967)*:

Arab socialism is diametrically at variance with European social democracy, particularly from the practical point of view, inasmuch as our socialism finds its level with societies not as yet developed in the political and economic spheres.[24]

Socialism, a phase that developed from capitalism both historically and philosophically, was coupled in Europe with the gradual rise of the industrial system. In Egypt, as elsewhere in the underdeveloped world, it is appearing

---

*Kamal Rifa't was an influential writer on Nasser's Arab socialism; he played an important role in the regime during the UAR period.

already in the pre-industrial stage, that is, during the stage of modernization.

The National Union was formally created in May 1957. In February 1958, a joint communique was published by Nasser and Shukri al-Quwwatli, the President of Syria, announcing the formation of the United Arab Republic. Following this, the Supreme Executive Committee of the National Union was formed, to prepare for the creation of an intricate organization for the accomplishment, in both Egypt and Syria, of the national anti-imperial and social revolutions' objectives. The United Arab Republic's elections of July 1959 were held to establish the "popular base" for the National Union—the organization of popular provincial, regional and supreme groups. The NU was divided geographically, into the Southern Region (Egypt), and the Northern Region (Syria). The party structure paralleled that of the UAR's government, and was almost indistinguishable from it, beginning at the village level, continuing through the town district level, and going up to the province or governorate, the regional congresses, the United Arab Republic Congress, and the President of the National Union.

This complex and cumbersome organization was more a blueprint than an operable and functioning mechanism. Thus, in describing and analyzing this intricate, web-like structure, it is not possible to identify precisely which organs were actually put into operation and which were merely on the books. However, in general, the supreme organs and higher echelons of the National Union structure were put into operation. The status of the middle and lower organs of the National Union ranged from that of tentative plans to ineffectively operating units.

At the bottom of the National Union pyramid was the Popular Base *(Qu'idah Sha'biyyah),* an elective body. This organization was intended to provide the key link between the leaders of the regime and the lower orders, and therefore to mobilize support for the regime. The link between the Popular Base and the party's upper level was to be the Local Government Central Committee *(al-Lajnah al Markaziyyah lil-Idarah al-Mahalliyyah)*. This committee was to consist of a group of ministers appointed by Nasser, the National Union's *Rais.*[25]

The Union's national organs were to be divided into three administrative areas: regional congresses, General Congress, and the Supreme Executive Committee. For the northern and southern regional congresses, membership was fixed by presidential appointment from Cairo. The regional congresses were responsible for reviewing both local and regional activities, each congress being headed by an inspector general who also directed the Ministry of Local Government. The inspectors general, Marshal 'Abd al-Hakim 'Amer for the North and Kamal al-Din Husain for the South, were appointed by President Nasser. To carry out its goals, each regional congress had 17 functional committees for dealing with youth, labor, women, public services, industry, finance, health, art, science and other fields. These were tripartite bodies which included representatives of local committees and various functional organizations, as well as the directors of regional departments.[26]

The national organ of the UAR's National Union was to be the General Congress *(al-Mu'tamar al-'Amm lil-Jumhuriyyah al-'Arabiyyah al-Muttahidah)*. The membership of this organization was to include persons nominated by the president and the regional inspectors, and persons nominated by town and village committees. Thus, direct nominations and ex-officio nomination were combined. The General Congress was to meet once a year at the direction of the *Rais,* and it was to be a key in implementing the three revolutions: national, Arab and social.

The highest organ of the National Union was the

Supreme Executive Committee. It was composed of the president, the inspectors general of the two regions, a secretary general, and the United Arab Republic cabinet, consisting of 18 Egyptian and Syrian ministers. The Supreme Executive Committee also linked the party to the UAR government. It was the United Arab Republic's highest executive instrument and that of the party as well.

The UAR government's middle level, the Executive Committee of the Governorate *(Lajnah Tanfidhiyyah lil-Muhafazah)*, was composed of the executive committees of district and town quarters and members of the General Congress. In the effort to have uniform structures in both regions, the UAR government dissolved the Syria Majlis (Chamber of Deputies) and set up one National Assembly to serve both regions. The dissolution of the Majlis effectively placed legislative power in the hands of the UAR's president, and his consultants. The National Assembly had no effective independent power; it was a creation of the executive, and essentially a ratifying body. The Presidium of the Assembly, however, must be taken into consideration in any discussion of policy formulation in the United Arab Republic, for the Presidium's president was Nasser's trusted friend, Anwar al-Sadat. Representatives from the army, from trade unions, and from Cairo's rival city, Alexandria, were also prominent in that organization.[27]

The Article Structure

Both the leaders of the United Arab Republic and the National Union ignored the letter of the law establishing the National Assembly's constitutional functions and powers. In a similar fashion, and with the same intention, to

152

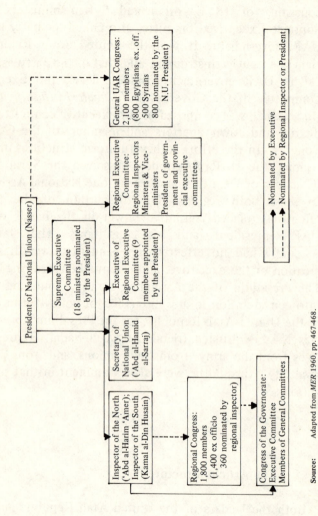

Figure 4: EXECUTIVE AND REGIONAL ZONES OF THE NORTHERN UAR REGION (SYRIA)

President of National Union (Nasser)

Supreme Executive Committee
(18 ministers nominated by the President)

General UAR Congress:
2,100 members
(800 Egyptians, ex. off.
500 Syrians
800 nominated by the
N.U. President)

Regional Executive Committee:
Regional Inspectors
Ministers & Vice-ministers
President of government and provincial executive committees

Executive of Regional Executive Committee (9 members appointed by the President)

Secretary of National Union ('Abd al-Hamid al-Sarraj)

Inspector of the North ('Abd al-Hakim 'Amer); Inspector of the South (Kamal al-Din Husain)

Regional Congress:
1,800 members
(1,400 ex officio
360 nominated by regional inspector)

Congress of the Governorate:
Executive Committee
Members of General Committees

Nominated by Executive
Nominated by Regional Inspector or President

Source: Adapted from *MER* 1960, pp. 467-468.

153

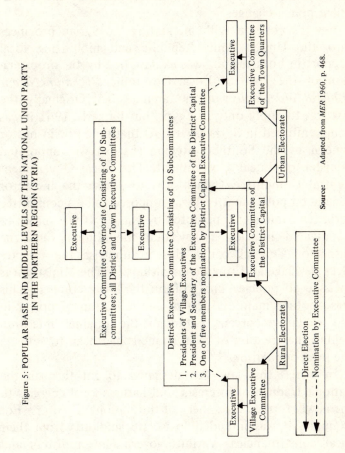

Figure 5: POPULAR BASE AND MIDDLE LEVELS OF THE NATIONAL UNION PARTY IN THE NORTHERN REGION (SYRIA)

Executive Committee Governorate Consisting of 10 Sub-committees; all District and Town Executive Committees

Executive

Executive

District Executive Committee Consisting of 10 Subcommittees

1. Presidents of Village Executives
2. President and Secretary of the Executive Committee of the District Capital
3. One of five members nomination by District Capital Executive Committee

Executive

Executive Committee of the Town Quarters

Executive

Executive Committee of the District Capital

Urban Electorate

Village Executive Committee

Rural Electorate

Direct Election

Nomination by Executive Committee

Source: Adapted from *MER* 1960, p. 468.

increase the importance of the executive, the members of the General Congress of the UAR were actually chosen by government nominations which had to be approved by the regional inspectors. Attempts at local and popular organization were thwarted by similar approaches and consequent policy changes.

Egypt's concern with integrating the Syrian provinces into the United Arab Republic and mobilizing local support in both regions was exemplified by the proclamation of the Law of Local Government *(Qanun Nizam al-Idarah al-Mahalliyyah)* in March 1960.[28] Originally, the law was to apply only in Egypt, but by early 1961 it was being enforced in Syria as well. At that time, the inspector general of the Southern Region (Egypt) was appointed Minister of Local Government. The Local Government Central Committee (which was to advise the inspector general on policy matters) was supposed to be a committee formed of ministers appointed by Nasser. It was meant to be divided in such a way that the Ministry and the Inspector General could closely supervise the directly elected village and town councilships.[29] The Ministry was to issue all policies, and to form the lower councils. This was another manifestation of centralization of power in the executive organs, although the original intention behind the creation of local councils had been to activate the local populations.[30]

In Syria, this law was designed to cut through the nation's traditional interests, and harness local energies to the newly formed machinery of the National Union.[31] For example, it was intended to isolate landlords from their local constituencies. Various government ministers and journalists wrote articles in *al-Ahram* and *Ruz al-Yusuf,* to explain that the interests of the new Local Government System and the Popular Base were identical.[32]

The attempt at mobilizing popular support in the

Northern Region was unsuccessful, and conflicted with the aims and interests of the Syrian political forces that already existed there. Specifically, such policies hurt the Ba'th, which had promoted and supported the formation of the United Arab Republic. The Syrian elements initially favorable to union were further alienated by the Egyptian attempt to abolish party government and parties, which Nasser considered "Divisive elements [of] foreign implantation, [and] an instrument of the imperialists."[33] The very concept of the National Union as an instrument of unity above parties, created dissatisfaction in Syria. Because the Ba'th, Syria's popular Socialist party, was under attack, Nasser was forced into alliances with the conservative elements whose elimination had been the declared objective of the regime. Thus, as the socialist objectives of the Union were being stridently proclaimed, their actual supporters were driven underground.

In 1968, the *Economist* judiciously described the problems and failures of the National Union scheme:

The formation of the United Arab Republic in February, 1958, put an abrupt end to Syrian politics and also to the rather timid experiments that were then being carried out in Cairo. The new Constitution specified an assembly, but in terms so confused that even Egyptian lawyers quail at the thoughts of interpretation. The first sign of movement on this front was last summer, when both regions elected village committees of the National Union; these committees were then supposed to elect provincial councils which, in turn, were to elect a general congress. But the pyramid has been slow in building. The idea of weaving, from the outer edge inward, a spider's web of committee reaching to Cairo at the center could be attractive and even useful. The trouble in the United Arab Republic is that little gets done and even less is understood by the people concerned. Thus the villages, called upon to vote, voted for the same families who have always been dominant, and the web breaks off long before it reaches the center.[34]

Thus the instruments which were supposedly designed to break the chains shackling the poor to their traditional exploiters, were not used. And by attempting to impose a new unity, the Union actually created new divisions.

Neither the National Union leaders nor local government members had enough experience in organization—or, perhaps, enough desire—to forge strong links with the *Sha'b* (people). Education in the ways of revolution requires well-trained party workers and organizers. Nasser first tried to organize cadres four years after the consolidation of his power, whereas Lenin had started preparing "professional revolutionaries" as early as 1903, 16 years before he assumed power. Chairman Mao spent nearly a quarter of a century—from 1927 to 1949—enforcing an articulate and complex system of tutorship in self-government in China. While the National Union and the United Arab Republic lasted, Nasser organized no popular nuclei of support, failed to integrate Syrian elites and Egyptian cadres, and trained no future political officers. Thus the National Union organization remained merely a bureaucracy, with few links to the people, and Nasser's cadres collapsed before the creation of the United Arab Republic.

The Failure of Union

Egypt's failure in Syria was not purely administrative. Syria's people could have been emotionally and politically recruited to serve a central government which they saw as "their own," but Nasser's Egyptianized Arabism (which saw Egypt as the dominant power in the Arab world) found no response in a country long associated with Arabhood *(Al-Urubah)*. The Egyptian authorities and National Union officers soon faced opposition from the

Ba'th, particularly from its non-military supporters and members.[35] When the socialist program launched in Egypt was finally extended to Syria—against the protest of Marshal 'Abd al-Hakim Amer, the Egyptian Proconsul in Syria, the UAR began to dissolve. This Egyptian nationalization of Syria was the last act of alienation: within a few weeks the Syrian army revolted, and in mid-1961, the United Arab Republic came to an end. With the disintegration of the UAR, the National Union, which even in Egypt had been merely a paper organization, also dissolved.[36]

The Socialist Union: A Party in Charge of Economic Modernization

After the failure of the attempted union with Syria, the Egyptian regime launched a new program. The old "social revolution," and Egypt's attempts at territorial and ideological integration had also failed. So a new program of economic modernization was launched under the auspices of a new government party, the Socialist Union, and the new orientation was definitely managerial at the expense of popular mobilization.[37] (In other words, this was a party dedicated to the creation of economic and social cadres, rather than political or electoral mobilization.)

The RCC's failure to integrate the Muslim Brotherhood into the first mass party, the Liberation Rally, had caused it to consider forming a government political party. The Popular Socialist Party *(al-Hizb al Jumhuriyyah al-Ishtarakiyyah)*, which was advocated by RCC Vice-President 'Abd Latif al-Baghdadi, and Ikhsan 'Abd al-Qudus, the editor of *Ruz-al-Yusuf*, was such a party.[38] The total failure of the second mass party, the National Union, modified Nasser's conception of the type of political organization best suited to Egypt.* Thus the Arab Socialist Union represented a compromise between Nasser's conception of a popular party centrally controlled, and a cadre party supported by the masses.[40]

The new party was to be formed on the basis of two principles: limiting the RCC's control over the party, that is, narrowing the organizational scope of the party's top-level structure; and forming a permanent party base at the level of party activists, to give the latter significant political influence, particularly in the modernization programs, structures and activities of Egypt.

Thus, neither the popular base of the *Sha'biyyah* (People) the foundation stone of the National Union, nor al-Qudus's concept of cadres, was adopted. Instead, party activists were to be given some political leverage on the functional level, that is, regarding factories, public authorities and government corporations established to advance modernization projects.

Agitation had not sufficed to get the *Sha'biyyah* to work for social justice: neither the Liberation Rally nor the National Union had been able to base the state's power on the allegiance of the population's lower economic strata. Rather than continuing to obtain support from these strata, the new program, called "State-Ensured Justice," was to be directed from the top, with a minimum of popular involvement.

A new political theory was proclaimed: Egypt's socio-economic revolution was to be based on a state run by military men and technocrats. In explaining this new

---

*It is most significant that the term "political organization" *(Tanjim Siyasi)* was not used for either the Liberation Rally or the National Union. The Arab Socialist Union was the first political organ in Nasserite Egypt to be called a political organization. Later, the Liberation Rally and the National Union were both termed *Tanjim*, that is, organizations. The term *Hizb* (party) was purged from the Nasserite political terminology.[39]

orientation, 'Ali Sabri, Minister for Presidential Affairs wrote: "Historical experience has shown that the government is the most valid representative of the people where factors and politics have kept a broad mass backward, ignorant and depressed.[41] The new era was to begin with a campaign against vested interests and social injustice; in effect, this meant a more intensive nationalization program and a growing bureaucracy, protected by the regime, to manage the state-run enterprises and lead social programs. 'Ali Sabri concluded: "The emergence of a public factor in industrial intrepreneurship in this country, projected against the background of the national experience, of private business and its connections with the past, together with its role as an instrument directed at the disruption of the nationalist front was an inevitable consequence of the march of events.[42]

The junta now began to assume complete economic control of Egypt. The years 1952-1957 were marked by the military leaders' efforts to aid Egyptian industrialists and private entrepreneurs, in the hope that private enterprise could demonstrate vigor and initiative and thus enhance Egypt's industrialization and development efforts. But these efforts were to no avail, since Egypt's intrepreneurs were politically impotent.

Ten years after the coup the wheel had turned full circle, and the government was pressed by its ideological and nationalist commitments to turn toward a so-called socialist economy. Officially, Egypt's new economic system is a command economy, planned and cooperative. Institutionally, however, it is a mixed system, and O'Brien's designation of it as a centralized market economy system is probably the most accurate evaluation of Egypt's economic system since 1960.

The Economic Development Organization, which had been established early in 1957, was given greater authority and eventually became the major instrument for nationalization.[43] The new system's main objective was the creation of a technocratic-industrial cadre by the military elite. Muhammad Hasanain Haykal, Editor-in-Chief of the nationalized *al-Ahram* and one of Nasser's most trusted political pamphleteers, wrote in 1964 that the Aswan High Dam project was "one of the most conspicuous achievements of the July 23 Revolution."

The administration that Haykal praises is a bureaucratic one, that discusses its current problems in terms of need for new technocrats and managers who can implement the hopes of the poor, but without mobilizing the poor. Thus, Haykal feels that the immediate need is for a new and efficient technocracy to regulate the High Dam, the Suez Canal, and the Desert Reclamation Authorities.

Slight conciliatory gestures were made toward the people. To guarantee the loyalty of the new bureaucracy, the "supervision of the people" was entrusted to cadres. There were to be two levels of government, the cadres and the experts. The Socialist Union served to recommend carefully selected political candidates, later to become the cadres. Thus elections in the UAR would be handled by the only election broker, the Socialist Union, whose purpose was to determine the quality of candidates, their loyalty and their potential as cadre material. A Preparatory Committee was appointed to determine the method by which the Congress of Popular Forces would actually name the candidates; it was this committee which managed elections for the National Assembly. If the Socialist Union's primary aim was to form a nucleus of loyal and dedicated cadres, it has completely failed in its task. Since the Socialist Union was largely designed to eliminate old political rivals, it recruited politically impotent and pliable members, rather than establishing a cadre of dedicated party professional and ideologues. To secure the praetorian political system, Socialist Union representatives were selected on an occupational basis—thus isolating what were to be the cadres from their raison d'etre, the political "shock troops" of the Socialist Union.

The instrument established to prevent the activists from becoming an ideological-political cadre was the Political Bureau *(Hizbah Siyasi)*, which was not mentioned in either the July 1962 Charter or the December 1962 Arab Socialist Union Directive. The Political Bureau began as neither a party nor a cadre, but rather a group of super-activists.[44] The left envisioned the Bureau as a revolutionary cadre, but Nasser refused to give the Bureau his official sanction. In the end, it was neither a cadre nor a committee of activists, but a group of functionaries similar to the Executive Committee of the National Union. There were two levels of political domination: the functional level, handled by the Bureau; and the other, real level, managed by the government. The second level of government was the cabinet, and the governmental bureaucracy. Nasser selected his new cabinet in 1961, without consulting the National Assembly. This cabinet did not act as a committee of the National Assembly, as in the case of competitive party systems under parliamentary political systems. The Nasser cabinet became an administrative and technocratic body, selected and approved by Nasser and his close cohorts. With the exception of 'Ali Sabri, between 1961 and 1965, no member of the cabinet has possessed executive powers. The cabinet is only responsible to the Premier and, through him, directly to Nasser.

In 1961 'Ali Sabri was appointed Prime Minister of a corporate directorship which would control the economic ministries. His 11 deputies were directed to attract qualified professionals, even members of the old administration, by paying higher salaries. If the old machinery drew personnel from the "theoretical faculties," this one would draw from "the technical faculties." Haykal claims that 45 percent of the new directorate were engineers.[45]

Of the seven newcomers heading economic, scientific

and communications corporate ministries, six were engineers, and one was a chemist.

Thus, the technical aspects of economic modernization were made the concern of a professional bureaucracy; at the same time, the political modernizers were protected somewhat from the emergence of uncontrolled rival elites. These useful, highly paid professional directors presented no threat to the regime's Executive Committee.

Sabri's new cabinet bore some resemblance to the Soviet Supreme Council of the National Economy, the *Veshenka*. As an operational unit designed to administer the new economic system, the Egyptian cabinet, like the *Veshenka*, provided administration, rather than leadership. Sabri's cabinet was supposedly responsible to a General Assembly; while the *Veshenka's* successor, the Council of Ministers, was completely subservient to the Supreme Soviet. But the UAR president did not give Sabri's cabinet even the minimal autonomy that the Soviets gave to the Council of Ministers. Its only substantial functions were those of management. Egypt's Socialist Union gave birth to experts, not cadres; and the cadres were neglected, to the advantage of the experts. The ideological indoctrination of the experts was not the Socialist Union's primary function; the Socialist Union was intended to create and supervise the two types of elites—what Chairman Mao would term the Reds and the Experts.

Egypt's Socialist Union provided supervision, censorship and control, acting on behalf of the government to keep the economic modernization programs, technocratic machinery, and the new cabinet separated from the process of restricted political participation. The administrative-functional cabinet was directly responsible to the *Rais;* the representative assembly was also under his direct supervision. The policy of restricted political participation was a concomitant of Nasser's modernization policy, intended to slow political mobilization while promoting economic modernization and growth.[46] This policy was coordinated with the Socialist Union's policy of candidate selection. Originally, only people whose loyalty was well known could become candidates. However, the candidates were later selected by occupation, and again were carefully screened in terms of loyalty. Thus, in the 1964 parliament, there was a predominance of candidates who possessed skills and were engaged in occupations which could promote change in a modernizing polity.

Sabri's cabinet came to an end in 1965, when Nasser's old friend, the veteran Free Officer Zakariyya Muhyi al-Din, became cabinet head. Sabri's rapid modernization plans had been thwarted by tying down the government programs too closely to supervision. Sabri's attempts to combine governmental modernization with functional political representation did not fare well. In 1966, Nasser relieved Sabri of his post as prime minister, to concentrate on building the Socialist Union; and appointed an engineer, Sidqi Sulaiman, to head the economic-administrative and functional cabinet. At this point, the processes of economic modernization and been separated from ties with the political party. The Socialist Union still functions only as a representative of occupational and technical groups. The cadres have been replaced by experts and technocrats, and ideological indoctrination is no longer a goal. The cadres never served the purpose for which they were supposedly created; and were soon superseded by the "scientific" model of experts.

The Arab Socialist Union Between 1965 and 1967. Before 1965, the ASU did not serve as the mobilizing political structure of Egypt's growing bureaucratic elites. The political functions of the Liberation Rally, the National Union and the ASU were extremely limited and their social impact was severely restricted. Nasser's political structures served as governmental parties, to eliminate

opposition and to diffuse the Nasserite ideology throughout Egypt's masses. These political structures became ad
hoc instruments for resolving critical political issues
concerning internal, domestic and economic policies. The
Rais, and a few of his trusted lieutenants, dominated
without interference in the areas of foreign affairs and
security.

The relationship between the government and the ASU
became extremely complex. Each level of the ASU (see
Figure 6) was dominated by the respective governmental
structures, thereby ruling out vertical mobility. Control
was horizontal, but not total. For instance, between 1965
and 1967, 'Ali Sabri succeeded in mobilizing into part of
the ASU pyramid locals who were neither governmental
bureaucrats nor under the domination of their respective
echelon in the government side of the structural pyramid.
It is true that Rank A of the ASU was closed to the
masses, for it was composed of veteran FOC loyal elites
newly recruited from the Nasserite army, senior governmental executives (military and civilian) and the professionals—lawyers, engineers and doctors. This is the ruling
elite that we shall analyze in the last chapter of this book.
The strategic elite, Rank B, was appointed mainly by Rank
A and the Executive Committee of the National Union or
the ASU. The members of Rank C, supposedly elected
from below, were in fact appointed by Rank B. Thus, for
our purposes, the political influence of Rank C members
was nil. Since 1965, Rank B of the ASU has been widened,
and its political influence significantly increased; but Rank
C has totally collapsed. To make the political influence of
Rank B more effective, Sabri abolished the district
structure of the ASU and established a network of
functional units of factories, public authorities, and
unions. These were given considerable autonomy in the
ASU middle echelon level. Domination over the functional
units was by the Activists.[4][7]

The Socialist Union was designed to achieve Egypt's modernization and industrialization without popular mobilization. (The cadres do not threaten the expert.) However, this regime was structured to protect the current ruling elite of the military bureaucrats, scientists, technocrats and former capitalists.

The vague acceptance of so-called "socialist" doctrines on the part of the regime may be the result of a commitment to a managerial organization, rather than any commitment to a radical revolutionary position. Modernization and quasi-socialization were consequently pursued,

Figure 6:
ASU–REGIME SYSTEM OF CONTROL

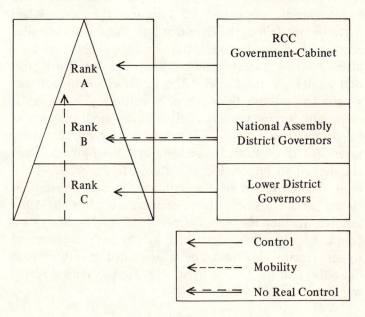

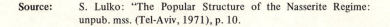

Source: S. Lulko: "The Popular Structure of the Nasserite Regime: unpub. mss. (Tel-Aviv, 1971), p. 10.

so that this class of managers could adapt itself to a postcolonial era, remain in power during the process, and guide Egypt in an antiliberal direction. This group has been aware that its political fortunes lie in directions different from those of Egypt's historical middle class; its commitments and expectations were governed by an astute evaluation of the sources of power in postcolonial developing states. Thus, it has introduced a form of socialism that is adaptable to bureaucratic and etatist practices.[48]

When the search for political solutions on the Arab level failed, Egypt's hope for the future took the form of a classless system, administered by inflated bureaucracies. Rather than attempting to build webs of political relationships and loyalties, Egypt tried to build an organization. Egypt was searching for political utopianism, in attempting to amalgamate the people of Syria into the union. When that attempt failed, the Egyptian bureaucrats and planners returned to Cairo to concentrate on Egypt. This time they offered a new bureaucratic model meant only for Egypt; that model was the Socialist Union. Sabri and his activists sought to establish their regime's legitimacy in the ASU, eventually turning the latter into a Soviet-model party, and to eliminate the political content of government structures like the National Assembly and the Cabinet. They also hoped to infiltrate if not eliminate the RCC, and to limit the influence of the military. It was hoped that Nasser would support these orientations after the 1967 disaster. In fact the period from 1967 to Nasser's death could be accurately described as the radicalization of Egypt. During this time, the ASU gained in influence, as did Sabri and his ASU activists. But Egypt's radical period was not to last for long.

6. THE PERSISTENCE OF NASSERISM: THE MILITARY VS. THE ASU

The ASU and the Radicalization of Egypt: 1967-1971

The military debacle of 1967 had serious effects on Egypt's military establishment. 'Amer's "suicide" and the resultant purge in the high command, intelligence network and war office did not enhance the reputation or the influence of the military professionals. Not until Sadat staged his countercoup in May 1971 did the military establishment regain its pre-1967 influence, if not its former reputation.

'Ali Sabri, the shrewd secretary general of the Arab Socialist Union, sought to use the military's ill repute during the postwar interregnum to advance his personal cause. To implement his technocratic and revolutionary programs, Sabri planned to enhance the role of his activists, the steering groups *(jama'at qiyadiyyah)* in the state, and to turn the ASU into a power source through the judicious management of economic production.

The slogan, "Transformation toward Socialism," was coined to describe the ASU's primary goal and Egypt's tactical goal. The idea was to blend the ASU with governmental functions, thus accumulating political power via the economic modernization of Egypt, by combining control over the governmental bureaucracy and economic technology with the "tutorship" of the ASU. In fact, Sabri's design was simply to wrest political power away from the praetorians, and eventually to leave the government with only a minor functioning role, such as managing the Post Office or the Department of Health.

The struggle for power between the praetorians, allied with the governmental bureaucracy and supported by Nasser, and the ASU, led by Sabri and his technocratic-intellectual allies, was clearly demonstrated in the debate over the drafting of a permanent constitution for the UAR. The provisional constitution proposed in 1964 was finally drafted in 1966. The ASU Charter of 1962, rather than the provisional constitution, served as the focus for political struggle between the two Egyptian viewpoints. The debate over the provisional constitution was conducted in the ASU and the National Assembly, and centered around the meaning of "true democracy" and "social democracy," which the ASU Charter labeled the basic law of Egyptian Arab Socialism.

From the start, Sabri and his allies tried to blur the distinction between a UAR Constitution and the 1962 ASU Charter. The praetorians' chief spokesman, Haykal, welcomed the involvement of ASU organs in the UAR's constitutional drafting process but challenged their efforts to radicalize the constitution by incorporating their own principles into it. This debate went unresolved, mainly because it was irrelevant to the constitution's primary purpose, of establishing a *Grundgesatz* (fundamental law) for the UAR. All this became obvious in the debate over the ASU's "authority," and the relationship between the

ASU and the UAR. The Sabri group sought to establish the political legitimacy of the UAR in the ASU, following the Leninist structural model, in which the Communist Party is superior to the state administration/government. The opposition, the defenders of "strict legalism," sought to differentiate clearly the "Constitution" from the "charter." Sovereignty, they argued, rests with the people, not the party, and the UAR represents the people. The Sabri group argued that sovereignty should lie with the ASU. At issue was the role of the National Assembly: should it be regarded as a parliamentary-legislative body, or an instrument of the ASU? Although this issue was consistently avoided, the debate was actually academic in nature, since a praetorian, patrimonial and bureaucratic Egypt was underrepresented in these group associations and in party politics.

This debate represented the struggle between two bureaucratic orientations: the praetorian and the technocratic. Although they were not so completely distinct as it seemed from the debate, these two struggling Egyptian elites were significantly divided from one another. The typical flavor of the debate was characterized by the struggle of the contending advocates trying to define the terms "people" and "social forces." The groups defined as the "people" included workers and peasants; 50 percent of the UAR's National Assembly was to be made of this group. The "social forces" were composed of workers, fellahin, intellectuals, national capitalists, professionals and local capitalists. Yet the National Assembly and the ASU were hardly representative of real socioeconomic forces. They only represented various elites of modernization, the bureaucracy and the military. Since no independent associations or political groups were permitted in Egypt, how could the UAR National Assembly or the ASU truly represent "social forces" or "people"?

As the only state organization bound by a set of written

rules (the 1962 Charter), the ASU was officially designated as the mobilizer of the "Egyptian revolution." Sabri's far-reaching reorganization of the ASU at the end of 1965 reflected the above debate. He intended to make the ASU into the source for political legitimacy in the UAR, and eventually the dominant party in the National Assembly, the bureaucracy and the government. The ASU was to radicalize Egypt and to create a power base and an elite structure that would present an alternative to the praetorian-bureaucratic-military cabal surrounding the Rais. For that purpose, the reorganization of the ASU's structure became Sabri's main task.

After 1965, the major reforms in the ASU were made in its Central Executive Committee. Previously dependent on the National Assembly, the Central Executive Committee had been "liberated" by Sabri, and assigned the functions of leading the movement of national struggle and mobilizing all resources for an equal and just society, eliminating class differences and transforming society. Popular and political control and planning departments were created around the Central Executive Committee. Each UAR governorate was to have an executive office, that is, a Sabri-oriented cadre, designed to avoid the perfunctory role of the UAR's National Assembly. The Central Executive Committee was composed of 150 leading workers, peasants and intellectuals. But real power was reserved for the Secretariat of the ASU and the newly-formed party cadres, the Steering Groups or Activists. This innovation challenged the Nasserite concept of the political party's role in Egypt. Nasser adamantly opposed the concept of cadres. Sabri, however, first introduced them at the highest party level, the governorate. Then it was put into effect at lower party levels, the factory and production units. The first group of cadres were comprised of worker-employee production units, designed to increase productivity. Actually this was an attempt to recruit technocrats, engineers, skilled workers and active leaders into industry, to serve as an alternative elite to the Civil Service and the government-appointed bureaucrats.[1] Sabri admitted, in an interview in *al-Ahram:* "The function of the ASU in production and service organizations [industrial and other branches of the public sector] was eventually political work."[2] Thus, members of the production units were selected not only on their technical merit, but also largely on the basis of their political activity. The Central ASU Executive Officers were to recruit prominent members of production units for the Steering Groups. The Cairo governorate, with the most powerful ASU branch, was the prime choice of most loyal Activists. In addition, a Socialist Youth organization (a comsomol) was founded by the ASU Secretariat in 1966. This clearly was designed to recruit students, intellectuals and radicals to the ASU.

The major reform initiated by Sabri and the post-1967 ASU was the reorganization and streamlining of the Public Sector. The Public Sector of the Egyptian economy was set up in 1961. It consisted of 367 public companies directing industry, agriculture and services. Since they had proved inefficient and not service or production oriented, a Supreme Control Committee, headed by Marshal 'Amer, was established in 1967. Sabri's production unit was then directed to wrest control of the vital Public Sector from 'Amer. He did this by making the ASU Steering Groups responsible for the Public Sector's corporations. Politically, Sabri directed his efforts toward dominating the production unit, to make it into a tool for influencing the direction of socialism in Egypt, and controlling the skilled workers' reservoir of elites.

Following the 1967 debacle, the debate over the ASU's future became more intense and better publicized. Members of the left wing of the ASU, represented by

Tali'ah magazine, openly attacked Haykal, who represented Nasser's concept of the political party "type." A lead
article in *Tali'ah* denounced the editor of *al-Ahram*
(Haykal) for following a bourgeois, rather than a revolutionary, path. This essay, although written by leftists in
the ASU, represented the most articulate view of the
supporters of a cadre-revolutionary and mass party. A
special issue of *Tali'ah,* on the "Internal Reforms of
Egypt," was published in 1967. It advocated that: the
leadership of the country, dominated by the military and
the class of educated, middle and petit bourgeois, should
be renounced; a party of class struggle, not a party that
institutionalizes the Nasserite military praetorian class,
should be formed; the new party should revamp the
praetorians by moving to the countryside, to create an
alternative elite; and capital should be nationalized.

Who, then, could save the masses and bring the party
back to the road toward socialism? The progressive class
(Rank B on the figure) and the middle class in charge of
national capital (the middle echelon of the ASU), in
alliance with the representatives of the workers, led by the
functional elites of the ASU. Although the ASU's left wing
still felt ambivalent about the role of the so-called middle
class, they also felt that a democratic regime must be based
on the masses from which the vanguard will spring.[3] The
Tali'ah group, in short, advocated a Leninist type of
vanguard party, in the style of the old Bolsheviks.

Nasser and Haykal rebutted that the problem is not who
controls the means of production so much as how
production proceeds. They felt that the control of the
means of production should be bureaucratic and functional, prototypes must be set for mobilizing the masses
toward production rather than political action, the need is
for unity of ranks, not class divisiveness, and the ASU
must remain a mass party controlled by a responsible

political organ (the RCC-Cabinet). To them, the "ASU seems from time to time a focus for power, a government above a government. This is wrong. ASU cannot and should not compete with the government." The political structure of ASU, they felt, "confused people and moved them away from real organizational work." The ASU created new leadership groups whose function must broaden "contextually"—that is, within the framework of a mass government-dominated party. "The ASU is and must be under Nasser's direct control." But, at the same time, the "new leadership learns from secondary sources on ASU work with the masses."[4]

Here we find a considerable modification of Nasser-Haykal's original concept of the ASU. New leadership means cooperation between the Activists and the bureaucrats. In fact, Nasser's speech to militant workers on the Helwan steel center represented a further amended view of the ASU, demonstrating the tacit influence of *Tali'ah,* and again reminding the military of its "failure" in 1967. First he reminded his audience that "we have succeeded in eliminating the 'power' positions which influenced Egypt before 1967." The reference here is clearly to the pre-1967 military clique responsible for the debacle. Nasser called for an alliance of intellectuals and soldiers with the workers and peasants. His position on the role of the ASU and the relations of power between the two "focuses" was modified by qualifying the alliance, saying that "the peasants and the workers were the important partner of a national alliance." But he "would not say that they have a privileged position . . . the revolution and development need its two segments [intellectuals/soldiers and peasants/workers] for Revolution [the first] and the revolutionary Regime [the second] are co-existent."[5]

The "Egyptian Revolution" is no longer represented by an alliance of the governmental reformist bureaucracy and the Revolutionary Action Group of the ASU. The ASU is not a worker-peasant party; it is a national party for all non-exploiting classes. "ASU is not a political party. It is not a wide and open mass party." Here the old Nasserist concept of party still prevails.[6]

The rest of Nasser's speech is worth paraphrasing, for it clearly represents his amended view of party. According to Nasser, the ASU is a front open to all numbers (that is the mass concept). He believes that no political tasks will burden the ASU (against the vanguard concept). Thus, the basic difference between the ASU and the vanguard party concept is that the ASU is an administration preparing a revolution, while the vanguard party is preparing to sustain it. Nasser says that this organization must include consolidation of Nasser's revolutionary leadership, erasure of the traces of the 1967 Israeli imperialist aggression, reorganization of regime and state administration, protection of revolutionary achievements (such as land reform and industrialization), cancellation of privileges given to some classes (for example, the military before 1967), reorganization of the army, making it a strong national army (with no meddling of the ASU in military affairs), mobility of high positions and top jobs for the masses, Arab unity, positive neutralism, aid to peaceful nations and friendship with socialist nations (primarily the USSR), and unity of the Arab masses.

But, Nasser concludes, any alternative party, such as the ASU, will be the party of reaction, and will represent privileged interests. As workers we do not want a workers' party or a proletarian dictatorship [referring to the vanguard party]; nor do we want the dictatorship of the toilers; since the party that would emerge in such a case [a cadre-oriented vanguard type party] would represent a false democracy.

The Military vs. the ASU[7]

The rise of the Arab Socialist Union after 1962, and of Sabri and his Activists after 1965, clearly threatened the military-bureaucratic group which had governed Egypt since 1954. Nasser acted as a superpolitical organ under whose supervision several political structures operated, interacting only through the president. Although he manipulated the political structures under his rule, he also allowed considerable independence to the ASU and the Activists. This practice continued so long as no structural or institutional liaison was established between the three bureaucracies of power: the military, the government and the Arab Socialist Union. Nasser served as chief and final arbiter of these three power structures, allowing no cabal.

The group espousing Nasser's concept of rule and of political organization was well represented in the governmental bureaucracy and in the military establishment. Nasserized and professionally oriented, the army was supervised on behalf of Nasser by Marshal 'Amer. 'Amer, a devout Muslim and the traditionalist son of a prominent village *Umdah*, Sheikh 'Ali 'Amer, was also related to Faruq's former Chief of Staff, General Muhammad Khaider Pasha, Egypt's Minister of War during the 1948 war.[8] In patrimonial-sultanist fashion, he acted in two capacities. He was "Father-in-Chief" of the army.[9] In this capacity he demonstrated his dedication to the individual welfare of the officers, many of whom he knew personally. He frequently presented their personal grievances before Nasser, who often consulted with him about army matters. 'Amer also acted as chief military spy overseeing the political behavior of the Officer Corps, discouraging deviant political inclinations and pushing for a strictly military professionalist orientation among Egypt's officer class. Since 1962, he had succeeded in gaining a "measure of independence from President Nasser in military matters, and . . . an ongoing struggle for control of the War Ministry had raged between them."[10]

This military clique was extremely influential until 1963, when the military debacle in Yemen caused Nasser to lose some of his confidence in the army. In its turn, the army felt a desperate need to restore the Rais's confidence in them and Marshal 'Amer played a key role in this effort.

The unsettled UAR and Yemeni affairs left the army professionals without an historical *lebensraum,* except for Israel. Their newly gained power was being challenged by an army of civilians who entered the arena of power through the various stages of party formation, cabinet making and election managing connected with the expanded ASU. The 1962 ASU helped increase the role of a new generation of bureaucrats, technicians, diplomats and party Secret Service men. The civilian branch of the government, although clustered mainly in the Arab Socialist Union and the National Assembly, was becoming highly represented in the Cabinet, the Senior Civil Service and even in the presidential office (formerly the RCC council).

Late in 1966, the military faction, led by Marshal 'Amer, Shams al-Din Badran and Salah Nasser and supported by Anwar al-Sadat, began to prepare for an eventual showdown with Israel, first clandestinely, and later with Nasser's tacit support. They hoped that a well-armored Egyptian army could at least hold its own in a fierce military battle with Israel. And, in the absence of a clear Israeli victory, the military and the Rais could still claim a significant Egyptian achievement. This last battle of Nasser's may have been organized, curiously enough, without his personal inspiration, but with his full blessing.

This does not mean, however, that Nasser was not responsible for the decision to go to war in 1967 and for the subsequent debacle. The army cabal found the Rais to be receptive, although he was indecisive about the type of war to be conducted against Israel. Nasser made a series of decisions in May of 1967, whose cumulative output ended in the June debacle. War was only one of Nasser's options. Ideally, he would have preferred undoing Israel's achievements of 1956, dismantling Zahal's deterrent capability (the Israel Defense Forces or IDF), and closing Israel's access to the Gulf of Aqaba by measures short of war, such as a combined strategy of mobilization in the Sinai and international diplomacy, the undoing of the 1957 settlement. This would achieve the goal of 'Amer, Sadat and the intelligence community without requiring a military campaign.

But the expectations of Nasser's rule propelled him inevitably into the 1967 debacle. Committed to the dual goals of Egyptian hegemony over the Arab world, and the eventual delivery of Palestine from the Zionists, Nasser could not resist his military praetorian cohorts, or the Nasserites in the military. Although Nasser did not advocate a military *tour de force,* he did subscribe to a quick path for Egypt's destiny. He hoped to achieve at least the retreat of the Israelis to the 1947 Partition boundaries and all that was implied in such a goal, within his lifetime. The means employed by Nasser were many and varied: they included diplomacy, extortion, threat, bargaining and violence. Nasser's strategy was different from that of his narrow-minded colleagues, Sadat, 'Amer and Badran. He was a better politician, and exuded great confidence in his own diplomatic and extortionistic skills, which aided him throughout his reign. Nasser was aware that, in many ways, he was Washington's "Man in Cairo," the reasonable, rational, Arab Bismarck, who stood above the emotionalism of the Egyptians and the irrationalism of the Arab masses and the narrow-minded military officers.

Nasser was also Moscow's "Man in Cairo," a non-Communist, anti-capitalist progressive, and the transitional leader of Egypt's revolutionary democracy.

To other Arab rulers, Nasser's leadership seemed indispensable. (He had convinced some of them that, if they did not hang with him, they would all have been hung separately—by Nasser.) The Arab masses felt he was the reincarnation of a remote but cherished past glory. Above all, Nasser was a firm believer in the concept he made into a strategy: the war of attrition against Israel. The theory of attrition is based on a simple calculation of the difference between the value of life for the Arabs and the Israelis. Life is cheap in Egypt, burdened as it is by overpopulation. The Egyptian peasant, not his officers, carried the brunt of the war and its tragic consequences. Nasser imbued into Islamic culture the thesis of attrition as a natural law. In this, he acted not unlike Stalin, Zhukov and other Soviet generals and politicians, who subscribed to the dictums of Kutozov, that Mother Russia always wins in the end, due to the sheer numbers of her citizens. Nasser believed that the Jews would follow the pattern of the Crusaders. In less than a century, he felt, the Jews would have become isolated, deserted and weakened, and their non-viable Jewish state would eventually disintegrate. Thus, time appears to be the eternal ally of the Arabs. In Israel, the situation is quite different. Life in Israel is dear and, in the end, Israel will not be able to pay the price of human attrition that is comparatively cheap for Egyptian Arabs.

Armed with an Islamic worldview, Nasser recognized the psychological advantages of a war of attrition with Israel in 1966-1967. This was dictated by its "reasonableness," yet even Nasser could foresee that Arab rhetoric, his own speeches and verbal commitments would also have considerable personal and institutional force. Once the war of attrition became Egypt's natural law, military men of the patrimonial and vainglorious type would be comfortable in this atmosphere of Nasserism. Nasser guaranteed his American interlocutors and Washington entourage that he would not succumb to Arab rhetoric and begin such a war. The Soviets, who knew him less well, were suspicious of Nasser's thirst for military confrontation with Israel, but they needed him as a client, and were basically confident in his ability to harness the very forces he had helped unleash. But "Our man in Cairo" proved unreliable. The war of attrition and the Nasserite ideology had far-reaching consequences.

The concepts that Nasser emphasized in Egypt—radical nationalism, Egyptianhood, hegemony, empire and the revolution—were internalized into the expectations of elites whose reliance on Nasserite rhetoric propelled the Rais into action he might not have opted for otherwise. The aggressive elites, both civilian and military, espoused forces which in the end consumed the Nasserite mystique, and ultimately the Rais himself. By the last week of May 1967, Nasser was no longer master of his own destiny. His forces lay wide open in the Sinai desert; the UNEF (United Nations Emergency Forces) had been dismissed and the Gulf closed. Once violence had begun, Nasser quickly moved into international diplomacy. To wrest away the Israeli gains of 1956, he moved into tactics of reapproachment with the United States, inviting Vice President Humphrey to Egypt and hoping to send Zakariyah Muhi al-Din to Washington. Nasser also hoped to consolidate his short-term diplomatic gains over Israel. Persuaded by the military that they could withstand the brunt of the campaign in the Sinai for two weeks, he had to hope that the Israeli deterrent, Zahal, was checked and that Israel would not behave irrationally and go to war. Or, if Israel failed to win swiftly, the next step would be to persuade the international community and his allies to roll back

Israel to its 1947 borders, once Israel's 1956 advantages had been annulled. At this point, the military strategies of the aggressive praetorians and of the Rais converged. Israel, however, failed to respond to Nasser's strategy. Thus Nasser alone, as Egypt's supreme authority, was responsible for the 1967 debacle, even though he had tried to achieve by combined military-diplomatic action what the military eventually accomplished with a grand campaign.

The most significant documentation of the military's position before 1967, and the explanation for the action taken in 1967, is the extraordinarily revealing article by Haykal in *al-Ahram* of May 20, 1967, on the eve of the Six Days War.[11] "Israel will fight for its survival which is at stake. . . . What would be the expected consequences?" he asks rhetorically. Haykal answers that Israel builds its defense on the assumption of Arab cowardice, and on a policy of force. Psychologically, Israel establishes a policy of terrorism designed to frighten the Arabs. Haykal says that Israel feels it is a superpower when it deals with the Arabs; it feels that the Arabs are at Israel's disposal. Now, he continues, with the preparation for war, Israel is becoming aware that these myths are not permanently operative; therefore, for Israel, the closing of the strait of Aqaba is an irrevocable fact. According to Haykal, at issue is not simply the defense of Aqaba, but Israeli national security. Thus Israel must turn to war, and "there is now no alternative but a military confrontation between Egypt and Israel. We know that the enemy will inflict on us the first blow; what we need then is to act so that this blow is weakened and that its results are as little as possible." But, Haykal continues, we shall retaliate with a large-scale second blow (that is, using any army of 300,000 with modern Soviet weapons against a smaller army, with poorer quality weapons). He adds that these must be analyzed on the basis of our pre-1967 thinking (a reference to the struggle for power within the war ministry since 1962). Haykal also speaks of a "perfect" coordination of Arab forces which will give Egypt a chance to use "our armed forces for a direct confrontation with Israel and the permanent blockade of the Gulf of Aqaba."[12]

The 1967 disaster was Nasser's crowning defeat as a pan-Arabist; he paid for it with the future of modern Egypt. Egypt became a garrison state, with its modern industrial development among the Suez Canal in ashes. Close to two million Egyptians living along the Suez Canal became refugees in their own land. And the Rais was forced to become still more committed to Soviet military aid, and more subject to Soviet political pressure.

The 1967 debacle clearly separated the military from the political leadership of Egypt. The military felt betrayed; they thought that Nasser should have pre-empted Israel in the middle of May, rather than waiting for Israel to destroy Arab forces.

The 'Amer Coup and the Purge of the Military. The disaster of 1967 was primarily political. The major defendant should have been the Rais, yet in a typically shrewd maneuver, Nasser succeeded in laying the sole blame for it on the military. Not only did he save his own career, but he also finally purged the army high command, leaving it at the mercy of history, which called it the sole culprit of the June 1967 disaster.

Coming back to power after the purge, Nasser's domination over Egypt was more secure than ever. How did he manage this, and how did he purge and tame the military? Although there is no positive information on the leadership crises between June and August 1967, the following hypothesis can be offered, based on the best information available at this point.[13]

Nasser succeeded in turning the blame onto the military

because the latter were dependent on him as Egypt's leading praetorian. The Egyptian military had never acted as a cohesive, united, corporate body—either in peace or in war. In addition, Egypt's separate and competing bureaucratic structures could not agree on a common effort of strategy regarding the 1967 war; nor could they consolidate their efforts after the debacle. Each bureaucratic unit was self-serving and thus easily penetrable. The war ministry, 'Amer, the high command in Cairo, and the divisional commanders on the Suez-Sinai-Gaza fronts were unable to operate as a single unit. The upper military echelons and the senior officers were professional, non-interventionist officers, dominated and manipulated by a small but active clandestine political group operating at the top of the high command—including 'Amer, the intelligence community, Salah Nasser and War Minister Badran. The support for the military by praetorians within the RCC—Sadat and Zakariyyah Muhi al-Din—was important, but severely limited.

Also, the military, defense and intelligence establishments' only source of legitimacy, support and political power was Nasser, who manipulated antagonistic personalities, structures and competing officers. The military establishment's major source of support was obviously the praetorian regime. Thus, to turn against their praetorian-in-chief was a monumental and unwise course of action.

The history of the dispute and the abortive coup against Nasser between June and August 1967 must be explained in terms of the above facts. Nasser resigned from office on June 7, 1967. By the 8th, the issue of responsibility for the debacle was already being bitterly disputed by Nasser and his senior military-intelligence and war officers. The military leadership, presided over by 'Amer and Badran, demanded that the responsibility for defeat should not be collective, since it clearly fell on Nasser. They felt that he should resign and have 'Amer replace him. Badran invited Nasser to the Egyptian Army's General Headquarters in Cairo. He arrived reluctantly on June 9. At the meeting, Badran, 'Amer, Zakariyyah Muhi al-Din and some senior officers gave Nasser a choice between the following two options: to resign himself, taking all the blame alone; or to share the guilt and resign collectively with them. Nasser resigned on June 9, claiming on television that "I am ready to bear the whole responsibility." Mass demonstrations demanding his return to office followed this speech.

Retracting his resignation 15 hours later, Nasser forced 'Amer and Badran to resign instead. But then the senior command demanded a retraction of 'Amer's resignation. Thus, 'Amer was about to be reinstated, with the help of the military. On June 11, however, some 30 senior officers were dismissed by Nasser. This began a grand purge in which, according to Haykal, Nasser dismissed some 300 senior officers. Salah Nasser, head of Egyptian Intelligence, then organized the anti-Nasser cabal. 'Amer, working from his rural home town on the lower Nile, appealed to Nasser to stop the purge and withdraw the mass dismissal of officers. Nasser, however, continued, going on to dismiss middle and junior officers as well. At this point, 'Amer decided to move in. He began with the following political demands: extend the basic freedom of Egypt, reform the ASU, extend basic democracy, establish an opposition party, grant amnesty to political prisoners, and release the officers arrested after the 1967 war. Nasser rejected all these demands.

In August, the 'Amer plot matured. His plan was purely military: to take over the headquarters of the Eastern Command (Suez), the Armour divisions, and Camp Dahshar south of Cairo. 'Amer and his followers were then to arrest the key persons around Nasser—his military allies, the Presidential Office (formerly the RCC) and the

Secretariat of the ASU. But the plot failed. The same military that could not organize itself to fight a war could not organize now either, for the decisive battle with their own praetorian chief. 'Amer was "requested" to commit suicide, which he did on September 15, 1967. By October 1967, Nasser was in full control over Egypt again, just as he had been in the past. Not until the abortive anti-Sadat coup of May 1971 would the military intervene in Egypt's praetorian politics again.

The Deradicalization of Egypt. Although he had succeeded in recovering most of his political power immediately after the 1967 debacle, in November 1970, Nasser died a broken man. None of the Egyptian territory occupied by Israel during the Six Days War was either liberated or returned through international pressure on Israel. The Israeli air forces penetrated the skies of Egypt as far as Cairo, and paralyzed those of Egypt. Close to 120 Egyptian fighter planes were lost, compared to some 30 Israeli planes. Israeli raids into southeastern Egypt and the Aswan areas threatened Egypt's internal security. An Egyptian artillery offensive over the Canal was halted, and replaced by a two-month Israeli offensive. Nasser and Haykal admitted to the loss of some 10,000 Egyptian civilian and military personnel.

In August 1970, Nasser had to sue for a temporary ceasefire, which the United States forcibly imposed on a reluctant but also exhausted Israel. In September 1970, Nasser's protege, Yasir 'Arafat, and his Palestine Liberation Organization were challenged by King Hussein, who finally ended the Nasserite domination over Jordan that had begun during March of 1967. Significantly, Nasser postponed a vacation trip to the Western Desert in order to mediate between the parties of the Jordanian civil war.

Nasser's death did not signify the end of Nasserist military praetorianism. The struggle for power between the military-bureaucratic praetorians and the functionalist-cadre group ended with a decisive victory for the former. Let us turn now to the last phase of the struggle for power between the ASU and the military praetorians.

Such a power struggle was inevitable in Egypt. Nasser had left little or no institutional legacy. The legacy he did leave, like that of Muhammad 'Ali, was personal, charismatic and autocratic. Nasser legitimized one-man rule, in which a Soviet-style collective leadership could not take over, except for a short term. In the long run, the struggle for power over Nasser's inheritance and the governance of Egypt could be detrimental to Egypt. This kind of struggle could only have been triggered by another military disaster, such as the war of attrition against Israel. The intensity of the power struggle also depended, not only on the relative power each of the diadochs could muster, but on foreign patronage as well. Twice in the history of Egypt, foreign patronage was overthrown: Muhammad 'Ali overthrew Mamelouk and Ottoman dominance over Egypt; and Nasser overthrew the domination of the Court, British rule and American designs over Egypt. Since 1954, there had been little incentive for foreign powers to meddle in internal Egyptian politics. Nasser's greatest achievement, the ouster of foreign intrigue in internal Egyptian politics, seemed secure. Foreign patronage again became an important but not a key factor in the future of Egypt's regime. Nasser was the first Egyptian to rule over an independent Egypt. At Nasser's death, Egypt's political "right" and its "left" seemed equally strong, although the balance could have been (and finally has been) tipped by a combination of foreign power and army support for the new military praetorian, Sadat.

The struggle for power between the military and the ASU resumed intensively and vociferously as soon as the Rais was buried. Both foreign and Egyptian students of modern Egypt considered Sadat just an interim president. Few, if any, of them envisioned him as Nasser's true successor. After Nasser's death, 'Ali Sabri had seemed his most likely eventual heir, if only because he was considered Moscow's darling. Sami Sharaf, the ambitious Minister for Presidential Affairs and Sharawi Goum'ah. The new Minister of the Interior and actual head of most of the civilian intelligence system, were secret but serious contenders for Nasser's mantle. These two men were confirmed Nasserites, as was Sadat. Sabri, whose source of power was the ASU, could hardly have been Nasser's equal, but he did aspire to a one-man rule of Egypt. Although a Free Officer himself, Sabri rejected Nasser's military praetorian regime; nor did he support Nasser's pan-Arab hegemonial schemes, which he considered a burden for Egypt. A committed nationalist, he represented the only real alternative to Nasserite military praetorianism. Sabri and his followers opted for a one-party socialist state in Egypt, in the style of Cuba, Algeria or Eastern Europe.

The struggle for power over the presidency was set along the political and structural arrangements left by Nasser. Informal political power in praetorian Egypt was vested in the Rais, who shared his political power in a patrimonial-praetorian style with various formal and informal structures of his own making. After Nasser's death, the formal and informal arenas (or structures) of political power that had previously been manipulated by the Rais, seemed autonomous. Nasser had never vested extra-political power in any Egyptian political structures, but he did prefer some structures over others, and the ASU certainly was not his favorite political instrument. The ASU, he knew, brought together men and ideas whose political maneuvers would seriously damage his own regime. Nasser therefore opted for the manipulations and machinations of various political coteries, personalities and structures, although this was not always to his advantage, as demonstrated by the army's opposition in 1966. Although the ASU was a Nasserite innovation, it was a political structure which he did not trust. Thus, by recruiting into the ASU those people who shared his vehement opposition to "corrupt parties" and his distrust of leftist intellectuals, Nasser was able to make the ASU into an ancillary, rather than a central structure of political influence in Egypt.

The real source of power lay in the historical branches of Egyptian bureaucracy: the army command, the elite Secret Service networks and the top governmental Civil Service. These had been the central instruments for maintaining military praetorianism and Nasserite rule. Muhammad 'Ali, the brilliant manipulator of court intrigue, had left behind him a complex bureaucratic-patrimonial system built on informal arrangements that was too complicated for his lesser heirs to manage. Nasser left an equally complex system, made up of a streamlined centralist set of coteries, kinship groups and modernizing elites, and a vast bureaucracy and internal police system.

Sadat was not considered either the brightest of Nasser's army lieutenants or the most ambitious; otherwise, he would have been dismissed along with Nasser's serious rivals, the brothers Muhi al-Din and the brothers Salem. Yet Sadat was in charge of the central formal and informal sources of power—the intelligence community, the army and the presidential office, Nasser's private ad hoc cabinet. Three key figures, General Muhammad Fawzi, the Minister of Defense, Sami Sharaf and Sharawi Goum'ah, now subordinated to Sadat and in charge of the governmental system, seemed to be loyal to the Nasserite legacy. Outside the formal governmental bureaucratic and military structures, the only arena for political debate and constitutional procedure was the ASU, which became the stronghold of anti-military praetorianism. Led by Sabri and his aides; the party chiefs in Cairo, Alexandria and the rural areas; and by the cadres of leftist *al-Tali'ah* intellectuals and the managerial class in the factories (see Table C), the ASU seemed for a white to offer a solid alternative to Nasserist praetorianism. But, in fact, it did not.

The Sadat Coup of May 1971
and the Decline of ASU[14]

In order to trace the details of the abortive anti-Sadat coup, let us discuss at this point the significant struggle that developed from it—the three-cornered struggle among Sadat, Sharaf Goum'ah and Sabri. Here we shall analyze the personalities involved, the issues at stake, and the struggle over the political structures of Nasserism.

Personalities. The anti-Sadat group was divided into two parts: the Sharaf-Goum'ah group representing the Ministry of Interior, the Civilian Intelligence Service, the Presidential Office and the Presidential Palace Guard Secret Service system. Sharawi Goum'ah, a graduate of the Egyptian military college, was born in 1920. He was one of Nasser's chief military intelligence agents. In 1961 he was governor of the Suez district, a key modernization-industrialization area. In 1965 he became Minister of Interior, and was instrumental in the application of Nasser's heavy-handed internal security policy directed toward the suppression of free speech and the freedom of the intellectuals. In 1970, Goum'ah was responsible for suppressing the student riots in Cairo and Alexandria. Under Sadat, he accumulated considerable power by streamlining the various security services under his Ministry. Sami Sharaf, another Nasser favorite, had had little influence on Egyptian politics before Nasser's death. As head of the

Presidential Office, he began accumulating political power in alliance with Goum'ah. Born in 1925, Sharaf was a product and a disciple of Nasserism. General Muhammad Fawzi, a professional career officer, was Chief of Staff of the army until 1969, when he replaced General Raid, who was killed in action on the Suez by the Israelis. Essentially a non-political professional, it was Fawzi's family and personal ties with Sharaf that motivated him to aid the conspiracy. Muhammad Faiq, a career officer before he became Minister for National Guidance, was another product of Nasserism. So was Hasan Tal'at, the head of civilian Intelligence.

'Ali Sabri, the Secretary General of the ASU, was a former Free Officer and a leading member of the junta which in 1961 opposed Nasser's dependence on the historical bureaucratic-military intelligence system analyzed earlier. He was the leading figure of the ASU, and campaigned unsuccessfully for an increase of its power; for the political mobilization of Egypt and the formation of technocratic cadres as an alternative to the Civil Service military elites. Abd al-Muhsan Abu al-Nur, chief conspirator in the Sabri group, was ASU Secretary in Cairo, the key party branch. A delegate to the 24th Communist Party Congress, Abu al-Nur was an influential leftist politician. So were Labib Shuqair and Dia al-Din Dawd, key members of ASU's Central Executive Committee. These conspiracy coteries are characterized by their strong kinship and loyalty structures. General Fawzi is Sami Sharaf's grand-uncle; Muhammad Faiq is Sabri's brother's brother-in-law; Goum'ah, a boyhood friend from military college.

The Sadat group was represented by a crew of veteran Free Officers (Husein al-Shafi'i, Zakariyah Muhi al-Din and Mahmud Riad), and a pair of professional officers—Chief of Staff Muhammad Sadiq and General Sa'd Shazli. Mahmud Fawzi (the Prime Minister), the propagandist-editor Muhammad al-Zayat and Nasser's former spokesman Muhammad Hasanian Haykal, all supported Sadat.

The Issues. The following areas were at issue among the three primary groups involved here. Goum'ah and Sharaf concentrated on the accumulation of internal control; Sabri and his lieutenants advocated the building of a socialist Egyptian society; while Sadat, Haykal and the military "hawk" General Muhammad Sa'd Shazli advocated priorities in foreign relations over domestic reform. All three groups unanimously agreed on the importance of the "eradication of the traces of aggression," that is, the withdrawal of Israeli forces to the pre-June 5, 1967 boundaries. The groups also agreed on the goal of the "Liberation of Palestine" (a euphemism that meant either a war of annihilation with Israel, or an Israeli return to the 1947 UN partition plan); but they disagreed on the tactics with which to achieve that goal. Haykal, Mahmud Fawzi (the Prime Minister), and Muhammad Fawzi (the Minister of Defense) were willing to settle for diplomacy and, if necessary, a combined war of attrition and high-pressure diplomacy to push Israel back to its pre-1967 borders. Sadat, Sadiq, Shazli, Sharaf and Sabri believed in the immediate liberation of Palestine, and so they opted for the resumption of the war of attrition against Israel. Most of the ASU intellectuals and technocrats were willing to settle for a push back to Israel's 1947 borders.

Sabri, the ASU and the leftist intellectuals advocated a pro-Soviet political orientation. The *Tali'ah* leftists opted for the Sovietization of the Egyptian economy; with most of them advocating a Cuban-Algerian type of socialist economy. Goum'ah and Sharaf, the military officers, the civil servants and the propagandists (excluding the ASU, of course) advocated a system of state capitalism and a wide range of attitudes toward the USSR. All these groups were unanimously in favor of getting military aid from the USSR, although they were divided on whether or not Egypt should be allied with the USSR.

The Sadat-Haykal group represented Nasser's type of one-party system, essentially an anti-mobilization cadre. The Sabri group naturally fought for ASU autonomy, and for a widening of its political influence. Undoubtedly, it was over the future of the ASU and the nature of the Egyptian regime that the power struggle was most bitter. Thus, there was a titanic struggle between Nasser's praetorian system and the ASU's modified Soviet style one-party system.

The Struggle Over the Political Structures of Nasserism. This was clearly a struggle between Nasserite and Arab socialist-oriented solutions, even though it revolved around personalities inflamed by political ambition, served by kinship loyalty systems, and abated by different orientations on the major issues facing Egypt. However, the conspiracy also represented the culmination of an intensified army-ASU conflict, which was shielded by the Rais. The military group that pushed Nasser to the brink in 1967 was purged after that debacle, but their followers clustered around General Fawzi still harbored feelings of revenge for their detractors in the Nasser circle. Elsewhere, Nasser purged the Air Force officers in order to pacify internal opposition after the debacle. Nasser also purged several hundred other officers, but on the whole he was not harsh enough with the army. The military remained intact, despite the elimination of Generals Riad (killed in action in 1969), Fawzi, Mourtagh, Shazli,[15] and Sadiq.

In conformity with the ruler type of military praetorianism, Egypt's military professionals and non-interventionists remained on the whole unharmed. Only the military politicians were purged. Since 1967, the ASU had been in the ascendancy. When Nasser purged the army, he needed strong internal measures to keep Egypt from falling into a civil war. It was here that Sabri, Goum'ah and Sharaf became extremely valuable to him. The real beneficiary of the 1967 debacle was the ASU. Sabri frantically recruited cadres from the technocratic-industrial sections. He organized leadership groups in the rural lower delta, increased his general membership and spread a wide network over the big cities of Cairo and Alexandria. As governor of the Suez war zone between 1967 and 1969, he organized militia and national guardsmen, all into the ASU network.

The ASU leftist paper, *Tali'ah,* emerged from obscurity and became the stronghold of extreme leftist-oriented intellectuals and journalists. The daily publication *al Goumhuriyah* (The Republic), formerly a Nasserite stronghold, was infiltrated by Sabri loyalists with the help of its pro-ASU editor, Ihsan 'Abd al-Qudus.* Both publications attacked the praetorian regime, demanding a halt of Nasserite practices, and advocating the establishment of a true Arab socialist regime in Egypt, as well as friendship with the USSR. Three months before the anti-Sadat coup of February 1971, *Al-Goumhuriyah* joined *Tali'ah* in attacking Nasserism and the Sadat regime. Haykal became the chief target of this campaign. A bitter journalistic war was launched against *al-Ahram's* Haykal and, indirectly, against Sadat's regime. *Sawt-al-Arab,* the Cairo Broadcasting and TV system, a key communication network in Egypt, was dominated by Sabri-ASU loyalists Dia abu-Nur and Muhammad Faiq. It encouraged openly anti-regime broadcasts and anti-military propaganda, blaming the military for the 1967 debacle and calling for the formation of a People's Army-Militia-National Guard revolutionary army. The ASU became a magnet for all anti-Nasserite opposition. In retrospect, Sabri and his ASU associates

*Al-Qudus voluntarily joined his colleagues in prison in May 1971.

made a mistake in assuming that the ASU was a powerful, Communist-like party. Sabri thought that the powers of the ASU's secretary general had reached the height of power held by Communist party Secretaries in the Soviet bloc.

Sabri was aware that he had only limited influence within the army, although several officers supported him—and subsequently were arrested by Sadat. Of the governmental bureaucrats, he felt that an alliance with "moderate" Nasserites Goum'ah, Sharaf and company would be helpful. But here Sabri's political insight failed him. He failed to perceive that, although Nasser was dead, the Nasserite regime was not shaky. Thus he moved in an anti-Nasserite way, by turning the ASU into the central political and constitutional structure of the country, hoping that by packing its Central Executive Committee, its Politbureau and the General Party Congress with his men, he could outvote and outmaneuver the Sadat-Haykal group. When the question of the Egyptian merger with Libya, Syria and the Sudan (submitted by Sadat to the ASU Executive Committee dominated by Sabri) was voted down.[16] Its rejection did not represent an act of political power; rather it was a serious indicator for Sadat that a coup against him was in the making, and that Sabri was furnishing the constitutional case against him. Sadat turned to Goum'ah and Sharaf, who had promised their support (even though they had already made contact with Sabri's group). Sadat also met with the crucial military high command, both in its Cairo and Suez headquarters and received the support of the Chief of Staff, General Sadiq and General Shazli. Sadat also made contact with some 100 officers dismissed by Nasser after the 1967 disaster, who promised him their support. We do not have reliable information about what kind of support Sadat sought or received from the Soviets, but we do know that he was in contact with Soviet ambassador Virogradoff, and that he flew in a secret mission to Moscow four days before the coup. Meanwhile, Haykal, Prime Minister Fawzi and foreign minister Riad made contact with the U.S. State Department, hinting to Secretary Rogers, during his visit to Egypt a week before the coup, that Egypt was interested in restoring relations with the United States.

The Gouma'h-Sharaf-General Fawzi group also did their homework, by aligning key military Secret Service loyalists. The function of this group was to effect the coup and restore order; thereafter Sabri, the ASU and their communications network would assume political control. Their preparation was excellent; but it failed utterly. It failed because the Sabri group underestimated both Nasserite institutional political behavior and the conspiratorial aspect of military praetorianism. They underestimated the military's loyalty to Nasserism and therefore to Sadat, who represented Nasserism. What is more surprising is that the technologists of Nasserism—Gouma'h and Sharaf—also failed. This part of the puzzle was resolved when the public trials against the conspirators ended in 1972. It is in the nature of praetorian regimes that their political cohesion is low and their political alliances short. Thus, a broad conspiratorial network in 1971 proved counterproductive. Even if the Sabri and Gouma'h-Sharaf groups had prepared the coups meticulously, the cooperation between the two was minimal and short-lived. Thus, the primary mistake of the conspirators was that they planned too long and their cohesion was poor. Political groups and structures are easily penetrable by outside groups and, in this case, by the pro-Sadat Secret Service agents. Also, one can speculate that the Sabri-Gouma'h alliance was precarious and enjoyed little trust, thus leaving it open for counterespionage, which weakened its links, and eventually led it to be outflanked by the Sadat-army group.

The death of Nasser and the abortive coup against Sadat can now be identified as a watershed in Egypt's recent political history. A new pattern of Arab politics has emerged: the de-radicalization of the Arab nationalist movements and regimes. The great hopes of Arab radicals were shattered in 1971. The annihilation of the Arab guerrillas carried out by the Jordanian army between September 1970 and July 1971, and the demise of its radical splinters, triggered a change to the right within the Syrian Ba'th regime dominated by the 'Alawi officers. In both domestic and foreign affairs, the regime of General Asad is certainly more pragmatic and less ideological and virulently radical than was that of General Jadid. The abortive coup against Sadat swung the pendulum of radicalization from 1967-1970 as far back as the pre-1962 era. The ASU is no longer an independent source of power with claims on the source of Egyptian ideology. The new ASU is modeled on the pre-1962 ASU type. We are back to the "ideal" Nasserite party type. Anti-radical and leftist witchhunting has become Sadat's chief occupation, next to military preparedness for the next round with Israel. The debacle of the Sudanese Communists in August 1971 only emphasizes the futility of looking for an alternative political model to the radical nationalist praetorian regimes in the "revolutionary" Arab states of Egypt, Syria, Libya, Iraq and Yemen. The swing to the right since Nasser's death is still in full motion.

Nasser, the balancer between the extremes of Arab nationalism, the Moslem Brotherhood fundamentalists and the leftists, established military praetorianism as the triumphant model of "progressive" and "revolutionary" Arab regimes. Today there is a neo-Islamic, anti-leftist, internal nationalist particularism in Egypt. It is no coincidence that three of the four partners of the proposed new Arab Union are graduates of the Muslim Brotherhood.

Sadat, as we saw earlier (pp. 140) was, next to 'Abd al-Rawf, the most influential MB officer in the Free Officers club. In 1947, he was the chief liaison officer between Sheikh Hasan al-Banna and the Free Officers. The MB Colonel, Mu'amer Qaddafi of Libya, belongs to one of the most fundamentalist sects of Islam among the Sanusi Moslems. Colonel Numeiry of the Sudan represents in spirit and action the neo-Islamic style of Sudanese politics. Radical Arab particularism and a neo-Islamic revival in Egypt, Libya and the Sudan demonstrate that, although Arab nationalists have not become moderate, they certainly have become more pragmatic and cautious. The new Arab Union was designed to annihilate local leftist and Communist opposition to the military praetorians, and to provide an insurance policy against the USSR's succumbing to the machinations and hand-twisting of its unwelcome, but inevitable, leftist clients in the Arab world.

The new Arab union was at first expected to link Egypt, Libya and Sudan, but the latter soon disappeared from the anticipated union. The Egypt-Libya union exists on paper—and innumerable committees and conferences have been set up to initiate the new epoch—but it is constantly being postponed. I doubt that it will ever materialize. Qaddafi's cultural revolution and Islamic radicalism do not appeal even to Anwar al-Sadat, the former liaison officer between Sheik Hasan al-Banna and the Free Officers. Sadat prefers the 1954-1961 Nasserite solution for Egypt: to deradicalize Egypt of its neo-Mahadists. The difference between Sadat and Nasser is that Sadat appears ready to abandon Nasser's radical pan-Arabism; he has discovered a new ally in the desert potentate, the puritan Wahabi ruler, King Faisal of Saudi Arabia. Sadat is considering denationalization and privatization of Egypt's industry as well as decimating the rest of the ASU radicals with the help of the old desert ruler. Certainly the October

1973 war was targeted to converge with Faisal's oil war. Although Sadat conducted a suicidal military campaign, suffered heavy losses and had two of his finest armies encircled, the war still produced a political miracle. Egypt's forgotten and forlorn case became a center of international political attention and action. Buttressed by the oil weapon, the Arabs were able to isolate Israel from the Third World, Europe and even, to some degree, from the United States. Sadat reemerged on a praetorian platform: insuring that either by war or by rocking the delicate international balance of power, praetorian rule in Egypt would persist.

The Sadat-Faisal entente is supposedly Egypt's last political effort to use a new Arab anti-oil front to pressure the United States to force Israel to withdraw from territories occupied since 1967. I doubt that this is the only reason for the entente, and if it is it would not be very fruitful for Egypt. I predict that this alliance will last no longer than the UAR alliance of 1958-1961 or the affair with Qaddafi, an off-and-on romance since 1971. Sadat, in the Nasserite tradition, is above all concerned for the survival of praetorian Egypt, which in the end is threatened by Qaddafi's radical Islam and Faisal's conservative Islam. He may exploit the antagonism between puritan and neo-Mahadist Islam. But not for long. The aspiration of praetorian Egypt is to become a modern industrial and developed state. It cannot return either to Wafdist Egypt or for that matter to Qaddafi's new version of Mahadism proclaimed in Tripoli. Egypt will follow neither the course of the desert sheikhdoms of the Arabian peninsula, nor that of Qaddafi. The praetorian system is persistent; it will not surrender to old formulas under new guises, or turn Egypt back to Wafdism or the days when pashas and bankers reigned.

The failure of the conspirators and the success of Sadat

clearly demonstrates the viability of Nasserite military praetorianism in Egypt. Clearly, without the support of the military, Sadat could not strike at the left. Although Nasser was able to keep the military in the barracks, while running a patrimonial-praetorian regime at home, Sadat is unable to repeat Nasser's performance. The high command has always been political, but now this is more true than ever before; the praetorian regime depends upon the military to keep itself in power. It knows it can depend on the military to protect it from newly emergent conspiracies. But could the Sadat regime defend itself against a military-engineered conspiracy? I doubt that. I have argued throughout this study that the ruler type of praetorianism is not a model divorced from reality. Sadat certainly is a ruler type praetorian, but then so are the potential post-1971 coup makers. The victory of 1971 was not Sadat's. It was that of triumphant Nasserite praetorianism. Sadat's ambition, or that of his military successor, could be easily leveled. The attrition rate of any praetorian regime increases geometrically with the rise in the number of coups that take place. Since 1952, Egypt has not had the chance to experiment with any type of regime other than Nasserism. The 1971 coup once again destroyed Egypt's chance to try out an alternate type of regime. The Arab socialist state in Egypt has moved, now, even beyond utopia. A regime composed of Free Officers who are disgruntled personal rivals of Nasser's, but nonetheless Nasserites,[17] has been re-established in Egypt. Since I argue throughout this study that Nasserite ideology was not really Nasser's innovation, there has been remarkably little change in the complex nationalist ideology that runs from Pharonian Egyptianhood to pan-Arabist Nasserism. From Sa'd Zaghlul to Anwar al-Sadat, the political differences in Egypt between 1919-1952 and 1952-1973 have been differences in the type of regime: the former

was feudal-bureaucratic and the latter praetorian-patri-
monial and bureaucratic. Egyptian ideology from Kamil to
Nasser, like the Egyptian social and political structures
from the Wafd to the ASU, is still no guide to an
alternative political system in Egypt.

POSTSCRIPT

The Praetorians in Command

The praetorian coup that began in July 1952 and was institutionalized in 1956, is still not the spearhead of the Egyptian Revolution, or the dictator of Egypt's future, but—as one would expect with corporate praetorians—the consolidation of military domination, the defense of the corporate group and the maintenance of organizational autonomy enhances praetorianism. Nasserized and professionalized, the military under Sadat acts as is expected of the only dominating political structure, identifying military corporate aspirations with Egypt's national interest. Sadat's coup strengthened the military establishment at the expense of competing political structures. Furthermore, in perfect conformity with the historical tradition of praetorianism, the Sadat regime is completely

200

dependent on the support of the military. Thus, the military officers are now in a position to arbitrate and, in fact, to dictate Egypt's foreign and defense policies. The Generals follow the rule of praetorians: to defend the Constitution from the barracks.

The tendency of Egypt's leaders to gratify the military establishment has been evident since 1967. Although the debacle of 1967 was a major military failure, the Officer Corps paid a lower price for that failure than did the other Nasserite elites. Even though Egyptian officer casualities were high—several hundred officers were killed in the Sinai in 1967, and some 300 were captured by Israel—they represented less than 7 percent of the Officer Corps. The results of the military's first trial, in November 1967, were so lenient that Egyptian intellectuals and students forced a retrial. A second trial took place, but again fell short of severe punishment. In fact, Generals Fawzi (the commander-in-chief until Sadat's coup), Sadiq (the now-1972-deposed Defense Minister), and Shazli (the commander-in-chief after Sadat's coup) and the new defense minister, General Isma'il all held high positions in the Sinai campaign of 1967. But, instead of being purged, they have been elevated to the highest positions in Egypt's military and defense structures.

Since no praetorian ruler can conceive of domination without the support of the military, Nasser urged the Soviets to rehabilitate his army as the first national priority. The Soviets helped Egypt in two primary ways: through direct support, aid and advice by Soviet military personnel, which penetrated into the lowest military level, the battalion; and by establishing autonomous Soviet air units and air defense bases in Egypt. The first type of intervention, while full of Soviet-Egyptian friction, was not too painful. However, the latter type of intervention eventually triggered the sudden ouster of Soviet military advisors from Egypt in August 1972. Why was this so?

The formation of independent Soviet military units and bases deprived the Egyptian high command of its control over the strategic protection of Egypt. The implications of this situation for the Egyptian military organization were profound: Egypt's military had lost autonomy over the territorial defense of Egypt; the Egyptian high command became dependent on Soviet strategic considerations and options; and the Egyptian air force, whose morale had always been low, was rendered impotent when replaced by the Soviet air force. Four Egyptian air force commanders were replaced between 1967 and 1970, and the general command of the air force became completely subservient to Soviet political, strategic and even tactical decisions. Soviet advisors in Egypt were openly contemptuous of Egyptian air force performance and potential, and specifically refused to recommend supplying Egypt with the latest Soviet missiles and aircraft.

By challenging Egyptian military skills, orientations and hierarchy, the Soviets encouraged the revolt of the Egyptian Officer Corps. The Officer Corps could not tolerate external political control, especially when it was foreign and opposed to Egyptian military goals and purposes. Although heavily dependent on Soviet support in the areas of logistics, training and supplies, the high command resisted the loss of its organizational integrity. The fact that several Egyptian elites—bureaucratic, civil and commercial—were suffering from the widespread Soviet intervention, and that the Egyptian people increasingly resented Soviet imperialism, was not sufficient grounds for eliminating the Soviet military from Egypt. The ultimatum submitted by General Sadiq to Sadat concerning the imperative need to shrink Soviet penetration into the Egyptian military organization proved decisive. In a praetorian state, the praetorians dominate politics, and Sadat, unlike Nasser, was dependent on the military high command, especially after the 1971 coup. Thus, Sadat moved to gratify the praetorian coalition only reluctantly.

The 1973 war underlines my arguments. Although the Soviets continued to maintain the Egyptian army at a high level of military preparedness, the praetorians—not the USSR—initiated and implemented the war of October 1973. We have no evidence that the USSR encouraged Egypt and Syria to go to battle, but when they ran short of materiél, the largest Soviet airlift in history was executed to maintain the Arab armies' capacity to fight. The Soviets supplied their most modern strategic weapons to the Egyptian armies. And when they discovered that the Egyptian forces might be annihilated, the USSR threatened both the United States and Israel with direct intervention. As in 1967 and 1970, a ceasefire was achieved with Soviet support.

Praetorian rule is now firmly, if not legitimately, established in Egypt. It needs no Nasserite sanctification; only subscription to the dictum so succinctly stated by Nasser in 1953: the army must patrol society permanently.

NOTES

Notes, Introduction

1. Jean and Simmone Lacouture, *Egypt in Transition* (New York: Capricorn, 1958).

2. Manfred Halpern, *The Politics of Social Change in the Middle East and North Africa* (Princeton, N.J.: Princeton University Press, 1963), p. 261.

3. Leonard Binder, "Egypt: The Integrative Revolution," in Lucian Pye and Sidney Verba, eds., *Political Culture and Political Development* (Princeton, N.J.: Princeton University Press, 1965), p. 419.

4. On this see Guenther Roth, "Personal Rulership, Patrimonialism, and Empire-Building in the New States," *World Politics*, 20, no. 2 (January 1968): 203-06.

Notes Chapter 1

1. David Easton, *A System Analysis of Political Life* (New York:

John Wiley, 1965), p. 278. Easton points out that the belief of citizens in the legitimacy of their state's political institutions is "the single most effective device for regulating the flow of diffuse support in favor both of the authorities and of the regime."

2. David C. Rapaport, "Praetorianism: Government Without Consensus," (Ph. D. diss., University of California, Berkeley, 1960), pp. 14-15, defines praetorianism as a constitutional form of "government without consent." Rapaport's thesis provides an outstanding theoretical discussion of praetorianism. Although the present work follows Rapaport's definition of praetorianism closely, it emphasizes the descriptive aspects of the subject and foregoes discussions of constitutionalism, consensus and authority, which are discussed at length in Rapaport's study.

3. See Gino Germani and Kalman H. Silvert, "Politics, Social Structure and Military Intervention in Latin America," *Archives Europëennes de Sociologie,* 2 (1961): 66-67.

4. See Samuel P. Huntington, "Political Development and Political Decay," *World Politics,* 17 no. 3 (April 1965): 386-430, for a discussion of political decay in modernizing states.

5. See Nadav Safran, *Egypt in Search of Political Community* (Cambridge: Harvard University Press, 1961), for an analysis of the consequences of this lack of parallelism in the development of Egypt.

6. The transformation of the army rebels of 1960-1961 into permanent senators only confirms the persistence of the Kemalist legacy in Turkey, at least as of 1967.

7. Samuel P. Huntington, *The Soldier and the State: The Theory and Politics of Civil-Military Relations* (New York: Vintage Books, 1964), pp. 1-81.

8. Ibid., pp. 80-81, 93-94.

9. Samuel P. Huntington, *Political Order in Changing Societies* (New Haven: Yale University Press, 1968), p. 194.

10. Huntington, "Political Development and Political Decay," p. 394.

11. Ibid.

12. On the relationship between the Muslim Brotherhood and the army, see Richard P. Mitchell, "The Society of the Muslim Brothers," (Ph. D. diss., Princeton University, 1960), pp. 61-250; Ishak Musa Hussaini, *The Moslem Brethren* (Beirut: Khayat's, 1956),

pp. 125-30; Eliezer Be'eri, "On the History of the Free Officers," *The New East* (Hamizrah Hehadash), 13, no. 51 (1963): 247-68; Kamal Isma'il al-Sharif, *al-Ikhwan al-Muslimin fi Harb Filsatin (The Muslim Brotherhood in the Palestine War)*, (Cairo, 1951). Jean and Simmone Lacouture, *Egypt in Transition* (New York: Criterion Books, 1958), pp. 131, and Lukasz Hirszowicz, *The Third Reich and the Arab East* (London: Routledge and Kegan Paul, 1966), pp. 229-49, discuss the relationship between the Free Officers, Young Egypt and the Nazis during World War II.

13. See Edward A. Shils and Morris Janowitz, "Cohesion and Disintegration of the Wehrmacht in World War II," *Public Opinion Quarterly*, 12 (Summer 1948): 288-92. Shils and Janowitz demonstrate that the defeat and disintegration of the *Wehrmacht* was due to the collapse of primary cohesion.

14. Liisa North, *Civil-Military Relations*, (Berkeley: Institute of International Studies, 1966), pp. 52-57.

15. *Actualidad Militar*, 5 (February 15, 1966), included the following relevant articles: "Patria y Fuerza Armada," pp. 2-3; "El Ejercito y el Instituto de Reforma Agraria y Colonizacion," pp. 8-10, 37; "Accion Civica: Cooperacion en la Campana Antipolio," pp. 12-13.

16. See Eliezer Be'eri, *Arab Officers in Politics and Society* (New York: Praeger, 1970), Chap. 3; Uriel Dann, *Iraq Since Qassem* (Jerusalem, Israel: Israel Universities Press, 1969), chap. 1.

17. Huntington, *The Soldier and the State*, pp. 93-94, discusses briefly the conservatism of the professional soldier, albeit in nonpraetorian states.

18. Daniel S. Lev, "The Political Role of the Army in Indonesia," *Pacific Affairs*, 26, no. 4 (Winter 1963-64): 349-64.

19. Gamal Abdel Nasser, *Egypt's Liberation: the Philosophy of the Revolution* (Washington, D.C.: Public Affairs Press, 1955), pp. 32-33, 42-45.

20. Majid Khadduri, *Independent Iraq* (London: Oxford University Press, 1958), pp. 200-06. See Col. Salah al-Din al-Sabbagh, *Fursan al 'Uruba fi al-Iraq (The Knights of Arabhood in Iraq)* (Damascus, 1956), pp. 29-30.

21. Huntington, *The Soldier and the State*, and S.E. Finer, *The Man on Horseback* (London: Pall Mall Press, 1962).

Notes Chapter 2

1. Ibrahim Abu-Lughod, *Arab Rediscovery of Europe* (Princeton, N.J.: Princeton University Press, 1963), pp. 86-114.

2. For analyses of various aspects of Muhammad 'Ali's reform program see Gabriel Baer, *A History of Landownership in Modern Egypt 1800-1950* (London: Oxford University Press, 1962); Hamilton A.R. Gibb and Harold Bowen, *Islamic Society and the West*, vol. 1, part 1 (Oxford: Oxford University Press, 1950); Nadav Safran, *Egypt in Search of Political Community* (Cambridge, Mass.: Harvard University Press, 1961); Helen Anne B. Rivlin, *The Agricultural Policy of Muhammad 'Ali in Egypt* (Cambridge, Mass.: Harvard University Press, 1961).

3. Lacouture, Jean and Simmone, *Egypt in Transition* (New York: Criterion Books, 1958), p. 53.

4. Rivlin, *Agricultural Policy of Muhammed 'Ali in Egypt,* p. 251.

5. Ibid.

6. See Charles Issawi, "Egypt Since 1800: A Study of Lopsided Development," *The Journal of Economic History,* 21 (March 1961): 1-24; David S. Landes, *Bankers and Pashas: International Finance and Economic Imperialism in Egypt* (Cambridge, Mass.: Harvard University Press, 1958); and Rivlin, *Agricultural Policy.*

7. Lacouture and Lacouture, *Egypt in Transition,* pp. 50-62; and Safran, *Egypt in Search,* pp. 27-30.

8. Safran, *Egypt in Search,* p. 31.

9. Lacouture and Lacouture, *Egypt in Transition,* p. 54.

10. J.H. Heyworth-Dunne, *An Introduction to the History of Education in Modern Egypt* (London: Luzac, 1939), pp. 115-16. See the same work also for detailed information on numbers of students sent to Europe and their fields of specialization, as well as the number of kinds of European missions that came to Egypt, pp. 96-253, *passim.*

11. Ibid., p. 17. Most instructors in the military schools during Muhammad 'Ali's reign were Europeans, primarily Italian, French, Spanish and English; for a more detailed discussion of their careers, see pp. 96-252.

12. Ibid., p. 119. See also Morroe Berger, *Military Elites and Social Change: Egypt Since Napoleon* (Princeton, N.J.: Center for

International Studies, Princeton University, 1960); George Douin, *Une Mission Militaire Francaise Aupres de Mohammad Aly* (Cairo: Societe Royale de Geographie d'Egypt, 1923); and the writings of the Egyptian historian al-Jabarti.

13. Safran, *Egypt in Search*, pp. 46-50.

14. Ibid.

15. See Jacob M. Landau, *Parliaments and Parties in Egypt* (Tel-Aviv: Israel Oriental Society, 1953), pp. 73-83. In a new essay, Landau adds further information on the relations between Arabi and secret societies: "Prolegomena to a Study of Secret Societies in Modern Egypt," *Middle Eastern Studies*, 1 (January 1965): 135-86.

16. Lacouture and Lacouture, *Egypt in Transition*, p. 72.

17. Safran, *Egypt in Search*, p. 49.

18. Ibid.

19. Ibid.

20. The sociological aspect and concept of patrimonialism is found in Max Weber, *Economy and Society*, vol. 3, ed. G. Roth and C. Wittich (New York: Bedminster Press, 1968), vol. 3, pp. 1006-97.

21. Ibid., pp. 1013, 1014.

22. Ibid., p. 1029.

23. See Chapter 4 of this book for an analysis of the strategic elites.

24. For the most detailed analysis of the growth of this class see Gabriel Baer, *A History of Landownership in Egypt.*

25. Eliezer Be'eri, *Army Officers in Arab Politics and Society* (New York: Praeger, 1970); Morroe Berger, *Egypt Since Napoleon;* W.S. Blunt, *Secret History of the English Occupation in Egypt* (New York: n.p. 1922), pp. 99-100.

26. S.N. Eisenstadt, *Essays on Sociological Aspects of Political and Economic Development* (Hague, Netherlands: Mouton, 1961), p. 13.

27. Edward Shils, *The Logic of Personal Knowledge* (Glencoe, Ill.: Glencoe Press, 1961), p. 117.

28. These ideas are borrowed from Edward Shils's seminal studies on ideology and civility. See "Primordial, Personal, Sacred and Civil Ties," *British Journal of Sociology*, 8 (June 1967): 130-46; "Ideology: Center and Periphery," in Shils, *The Logic of Personal Knowledge*, pp. 117-30. A parallel interpretation of the role of

primordial forces in the process of political integration is given by Clifford Geertz, "The Integrative Revolution," in *Old Societies and New States,* ed. Clifford Geertz (Glencoe, Ill.: Glencoe Press, 1963).

29. Henry H. Ayrout, *The Egyptian Peasant* (Boston: Beacon Press, 1963), p. 113.

30. Gabriel Baer, *Egyptian Guilds in Modern Times,* Israel Oriental Society, no. 8, Jerusalem, 1964.

31. Gabriel Baer, "Social Change in Egypt," in *Political and Social Change in Modern Egypt,* ed. P.M. Holt (Oxford: Oxford University Press, 1968), pp. 135-61.

32. Ibid., pp. 154-58.

33. See discussion of agrarian reform in Chapter 4.

34. Baer, "Social Change," p. 135.

35. The best political and intellectual biography of al-Sayyid is in Jamal M. Ahmed, *The Intellectual Origins of Egyptian Nationalism* (London: Oxford University Press, 1960). See also Safran, *Egypt in Search,* pp. 90-97; on Mustafa Kamil, see 'Abd al-Rahman al-Rafi'i, *Mustafa Kamil Ba'ith al-Harakah al Wataniyyah (Mustafa Kamil: The Resurrector of the Nationalist Movement),* (Cairo, 1960).

36. Jacob Landau, *Parliaments and Parties in Egypt,* pp. 149-59.

37. See Gabriel Baer, *A History of Landownership in Egypt,* pp. 140-46. Baer points out that some of Mustafa Kamil's nationalist party central figures were also large landowners (see pp. 144-45).

38. Safran, *Egypt in Search,* p. 195. Professor El-Saaty discusses the difficulties encountered in studying social stratification in Egypt. We know of no attempt to use recently developed survey techniques to "discover" the Egyptian middle class. According to El-Saaty, the Egyptian middle class constitutes roughly 16.2 percent of the population (1947 census), 8.16 percent being rural middle class. This estimate may be high. See "The Middle Class in Egypt," *L'Egypte Contemporaine,* 48 (January 1957): 47-64.

39. Taha Hussain, *The Future of Culture in Egypt, (Mustaqbal al-Thaqafeh fi Misr,* Washington, D.C.: American Council of Learned Societies, 1954), p. 4.

40. Safran, *Egypt in Search,* pp. 86-87. See also the excellent discussion of Egypt's intellectual orientation on pp. 151-64.

41. George Antonius, *The Arab Awakening* (New York: Capricorn Books, 1965), p. 99.

42. Ahmed, *Intellectual Origins,* p. 97.

43. Ibid., p. 97.

44. Neither Mustafa Kamil nor his successor, Muhammad Farid, achieved the degree of political mobility which the Egyptian Civil Service had promised under Lord Cromer's reforms.

45. Safran, *Egypt in Search,* p. 140.

46. Charles Issawi, *Egypt in Revolution: An Economic Analysis* (London: Oxford University Press, 1963), pp. 82-86.

47. Safran, *Egypt in Search,* p. 140.

48. Richard P. Mitchell, *The Society of the Muslim Brothers* (London: Oxford University Press, 1969), pp. 524-29.

49. On the struggle over the Constitution between the liberal-nationalists and the modernists, their irresolution and consequences, see Safran, *Egypt in Search,* pp. 108-21.

50. For the most penetrating analysis of the demise of an Islamic constitution in Pakistan, see Leonard Binder, *Religion and Politics in Pakistan* (Berkeley and Los Angeles: University of California Press, 1963). For a new look into the Islamic state for Pakistan, see E.I.J. Rosenthal, *Islam in the Modern National State* (Cambridge: Cambridge University Press, 1965), pp. 125-53.

51. See Muhammad Asad's *The Principles of State and Government in Islam* (Berkeley and Los Angeles: University of California Press, 1961).

52. Binder, *Religion and Politics in Pakistan,* p. 3, clearly states: "Pakistan came into being as a result of the increasing democratization and Indianization of the government of India."

53. See Safran, *Egypt in Search,* pp. 125-40; and Ahmed, *Intellectual Origins.*

54. H.A.R. Gibb, *Modern Trends in Islam* (Chicago: Chicago University Press, 1947), p. 113.

55. In the 1950 elections, the electorate still supported the Wafd overwhelmingly.

56. On the composition of the middle classes within the Muslim Brotherhood, see Mitchell, *The Society of the Muslim Brothers,* pp. 524-29. On the role of the Muslim Brotherhood and the *Misr al-Fatat* in the army see Majid Khadduri, " 'Aziz 'ali al-Misri and the Arab Nationalist Movement," in *Middle Eastern Affairs,* vol. 4, ed. Albert Hourani (St. Anthony's Papers, no. 17), 1965, pp. 14-163;

Be'eri, "On the History," pp. 247-48 (English summary pp. xiii-xvi). Lacouture and Lacouture, *Egypt in Transition* (Criterion Books, 1958). See also 'Abd al-Latif al-Baghdadi, *Ma Kbal al-dubbat al-Ahrar* (On the Free Officers), (Cairo: Government publication, 1953), pp. 188-91; and Mitchell, *The Society of the Muslim Brothers*, pp. 530.

57. An Officer and devout Muslim Brotherhood member, Major Mahmud Labib, was sent by al-Banna to help the Mufti of Jerusalem during the Arab revolt, 1936-1939. When he returned to Egypt, he assisted a Brotherhood officer, Major 'Abd al-Mun'im 'Abd al-Ra'uf, in recruiting army officers and establishing Muslim Brotherhood cells in the army. After 1947, Labib organized the training and recruitment of army volunteers to aid in the Palestine campaign. Mitchell points out that Labib made contact with Nasser as early as 1944 (*The Society of the Muslim Brothers*, p. 150). The literature on this subject—Mitchell's study excepted—fails to bring out the importance of the Muslim Brotherhood's impact on the junior officers, and since 1954 all reference to possible connections between any of these officers, especially Nasser's group, and the Muslim Brotherhood have been expurgated from the official and semiofficial histories of the regime. Publications which deal with Nasser's successes ignore the activities of members of other groups, and exaggerate the similarities between their organizations and the original 1945 Nasser group. This is especially true of Anwar al-Sadat, but it is also evident in 'Abd al-Latif al-Baghdadi's Memoirs *(Ma kbal)*. See also various public statements of Kamal al-Din Husain in the Egyptian press of the time, and Mitchell, *The Society of the Muslim Brothers*, pp. 148-60.

58. Misr al-Fatat also increased its following during this time.

59. Safran, *Egypt in Search*, p. 243.

60. Mitchell, *The Society of the Muslim Brothers*, p. 504.

61. Ibid., p. 424.

62. Be'eri, "On the History," pp. 247-48.

63. Mitchell, *The Society of the Muslim Brothers*, p. 151.

64. Due to the lack of documentation on the formation of Nasser's Society of Free Officers from Palestine war veterans who wished to distinguish themselves from other Free Officers, it is impossible to give a more conclusive account of the attitudes of this group toward the Muslim Brotherhood after Palestine, except to

point out that the group seemed willing to cooperate with the Brotherhood, but not to be an instrument of it. On Brotherhood-Free Officers relations, especially those of the Nasser group, see Kamal al-Sharif, *Al-Ikhwan al-muslimin Fi-Harb-Filastin (The Muslum Brotherhood in the Palestine War)* (Cairo, 1951). Mahmud Labib's memoirs have not yet been published. See also Hilmi Salam's series of articles on the origins of the July coup in the daily *al-Mussawar,* October-November, 1952.

65. Lacouture and Lacouture, *Egypt in Transition,* pp. 125-60.

66. Mitchell, *The Society of the Muslim Brothers,* pp. 157-58.

67. For information on the Nasser-Hudaibi relationship, see Ibid., pp. 161-76.

68. Shamir, "Five Years," pp. 261-78.

69. *Al-Ahram,* January 1953.

70. P.J. Vatikiotis, *The Egyptian Army in Politics* (Blooming-ton, Ind.: Indiana University Press, 1961).

71. Sir Reader Bullard, ed., *The Middle East: A Political and Economic Survey,* 3rd ed., Royal Institute for International Affairs (London: Oxford University Press, 1958).

72. Eliezer Be'eri, "On the History of the Free Officers." *The New East (Hamizrah Hehadash),* vol. 13, no. 51 (1903): 247-68.

73. Some officers continued to resent the Nasser group between 1952 and 1954. Khalid Muhi al-Din's abortive 1954 coup indicated that the armored division, at least, was still disloyal.

74. *Al-Ahram,* December 9, 1954.

75. *Al-Ahram,* January 16, 1953.

76. Shimon Shamir, "The Question of a 'National Philosophy' in Contemporary Arab Thought," *Asian and African Studies,* vol. 1 (Jerusalem: Israel Oriental Society, 1965).

77. We must distinguish between Weber's and Huntington's definitions of praetorianism. To Huntington it is an analytic concept, while to Weber it indicates a type of domination.

78. Max Weber, *Economy and Society,* vol. 3 (New York: Bedminster, 1968), pp. 1013-31.

79. Albert H. Lybyer, *The Government of the Ottoman Empire in the Times of Suleiman the Magnificent* (New York: Russell and Russell, 1966).

80. W. Goerlitz, *History of the German General Staff* (New York: Praeger, 1953), p. 199.

81. Be'eri, "On the History."

82. For an excellent description of the Egyptian army, see Morroe Berger, *Egypt Since Napoleon.*

83. Ibid., pp. 206-10.

84. Be'eri, "On the History."

85. Huntington, "Power, Expertise, and the Military Profession," *Daedalus,* 92 (1953): 785-807.

86. R. Tignor, *Modernization and British Rule* (Princeton, N.J.: Princeton University Press, 1966).

87. Much of the *Ikhtarna Lak* and *Kutub Siyasiyyah* literature deals with the connection between Egypt and Islam. See also Husain Mu'nis, *Hudat al-Insaniyyah fi al-Sharq (The Guides of Humanity in the East);* 'Abd al-Qadir Hatim, *Ruh al-Dustur (The Spirit of the Law);* Muhammad Haqqi, *Falsafat al-Qaumiyyah (The Philosophy of Nationalism);* and Muhammad M. 'Ata, *The Islamic Call.* (All of these pamphlets are published in Cairo by *Ikhtarna Lak* Publications, English series, from 1953-1956.) See also 'Ata's *Nahwa Wa'y Jadid (Toward a New Consciousness).*

88. Gibb and Bowen, *Islamic Society,* pp. 70-71.

89. Wilfred Cantwell Smith, *Islam in Modern History* (Princeton, N.J.: Princeton University Press, 1957), p. 94.

90. The philosophic contribution of al-Afghani went unchallenged until recently. Some revisionist historians point to the subjectively oriented biographies of al-Afghani written by admirers, some of which were encouraged by al-Afghani himself. Thus, what actually amounted to pamphleteering has been since accepted as history. See Elie Kedourie, *Afghani and 'Abduh* (London: Frank Cass, 1966); Sylvia G. Haim, *Arab Nationalism* (Berkeley and Los Angeles: University of California Press, 1964), p. 6, writes, "Al-Afghani was the very type of revolutionary-conspirator and activist so well known in Europe in modern times." See also Nikki R. Keddie, "Sayyid Jamal al-Din al-Afghani's First Twenty-Seven Years: The Darker Period," *The Middle East Journal,* 20, no. 4 (Autumn 1966): 517-33; and Nikki Keddie, "The Pan-Islamic Appeal: Afghani and Abdulhamid II," *Middle Eastern Studies,* 3, no. 1 (October 1966): 46-67. On the rise of pan-Islamism as a challenge to Western encounters see Safran, *Egypt in Search,* pp. 43-50. For a balanced and a sympathetic appraisal of al-Afghani, see Albert Hourani, *Arabic Thought in the Liberal Age, 1787-1939* (London: Oxford University Press, 1966), pp. 103-29.

91. Haim, *Arab Nationalism,* p. 7.

92. Gibb, *Modern Trends in Islam.*

93. Rashid Rida, *History of Mohammad 'Abduh,* vol. 2, pp. 36, quoted in Safran, *Egypt in Search,* p. 63.

94. Safran, *Egypt in Search,* p. 70.

95. Ibid., p. 84.

96. Malcolm H. Kerr, *Islamic Reform* (Berkeley and Los Angeles: University of California Press, 1966), p. 1.

97. See Gibb, *Modern Trends in Islam,* p. 104. On apologetics, see also Smith, *Islam in Modern History;* and von Grunebaum, *Modern Islam: The Search for Cultural Identity* (Berkeley and Los Angeles: University of California Press, 1962).

98. Gibb, *Modern Trends in Islam,* p. 103.

99. Ibid., p. 104.

100. Ibid., p. 107.

101. For penetrating analysis of new Arabist apologetics in the guise of nationalist philosophy, see Shamir, "The Question," pp. 40-41.

102. Mitchell, *The Society of Muslim Brothers,* pp. 374-82.

103. Ibid., p. 354.

104. Nasser, *Egypt's Liberation.*

105. Kamal al-Din Husain, Introduction to 'Abd al-Star Kamal, *Misr al-'Uzma* (Mighty Egypt), (Cairo: *Ikhtarna Lak,* 1954), pp. 3-4.

106. Nasser, *Egypt's Liberation,* p. 12.

107. Nasser, Introduction to Husain Mu'nis, *Egypt and Its Mission* (Cairo: *Ikhtarna Lak,* no. 55, 1956?), pp. 5-8. See also I. Oron "The Nationalist Myth of Egypt," *New East,* 40 (1960), pp. 164-66.

108. The magazine *Ruz al-Yusaf* has dedicated itself to the most vehement anti-Westernism. The cartoons on the cover usually depict a despicable, conniving fat Uncle Sam or Colonel Blimp wearing a hat on which the star of David is conspicuous. Articles on imperialism are the standard fare.

109. Nasser, *Egypt's Liberation,* pp. 50-52.

110. Nasser, Introduction to Muhammad M. 'Ata, *The Islamic Call* (Cairo: *Ikhtarna Lak,* n.d.), p. 2.

111. Ibid., p. 6.

112. Nasser, *Egypt's Liberation*, p. 88.

113. Mitchell, *The Society of Muslim Brothers*, pp. 405-08.

114. 'Ata, *The Islamic Call*, pp. 160, 161.

115. Al-Aqad, *Al-Dimuqratiyah Fi Islam (Democracy in Islam)*.

116. Mitchell, *The Society of Muslim Brothers*, pp. 425-27.

117. James Heaphy, "The Organization of Egypt: Inadequacies of a Non-Political Model for Nation-Building," *World Politics*, 28, no. 2 (January 1966): 193.

118. Sheldon Wolin, *Politics and Vision* (Boston: Little, Brown, 1960), p. 353.

119. 'Abd al-Rahman al-Rafi'i, *Mustafa Kamil*, pp. 392-93, quoted in Safran, *Egypt in Search*, p. 87.

Notes Chapter 3

1. Amos Perlmutter "The Arab Military Elite" *World Politics*, vol. 22, no. 2 (January 1970), pp. 269-300.

2. Edward Shils, "The Military in the Political Development of the New States," in John J. Johnson, *The Role of the Military in Underdeveloped Countries* (Princeton, N.J.: Princeton University Press, 1962), pp. 7-68.

3. Ibid., pp. 52-60.

4. Lucian Pye, "Armies in the Process of Political Modernization," in Johnson, *The Role of the Military*, pp. 69-89.

5. Manfred Halpern, "Middle Eastern Armies and the New Middle Class," in Johnson, *The Role of the Military*, p. 286.

6. T. Cuyler Young, "The Social Support of Current Iranian Policy," *The Middle East Journal*, vol. 16, no. 2 (Spring 1952): 125-43.

7. John J. Johnson, *Political Change in Latin America: The Emergence of The Middle Sectors* (Stanford: Stanford University Press, 1958).

8. Manfred Halpern, *The Politics of Social Change in the Middle East and North Africa* (Princeton, N.J.: Princeton University Press, 1963). In footnotes 3 and 4 on pp. 54-55, and on pp. 55-56, Halpern discusses the qualities of this new class, and comments on Young's and Johnson's evidence for the emergence of what Johnson prefers to call the "middle sectors" as a new class in developing areas.

9. Ibid., pp. 51-78.

10. Ibid., pp. 258-74.

11. Ibid., p. 54, footnote 4. See also Halpern's comment on pp. 54-55 that "among these two [Johnson and Young] and the present essay, there are common intellectual lines."

12. Johnson, *Political Change*, pp. vii-ix.

13. George Blankesten, "In Quest of the Middle Sectors," *World Politics*, 12, no. 2 (January 1960): 326.

14. Halpern, *The Politics*, p. 59.

15. Ibid.

16. John Harsanyi defines dynamic explanation this way:

When at least some of the explanatory variables used belong to an *earlier period* than the variables to be explained. More generally, we should speak of the dynamic explanation also if what we directly try to explain, and/or what we offer as explanation, involve not only the values of certain social variables at a given time, but also their time trends (time derivatives, i.e., the directions and rates of their change).

"Explanation and Comparative Dynamics in Social Science," *Behavioral Science*, 5, no. 2 (April 1960): 137.

17. Charles Issawi, "Egypt Since 1800: A Study in Lopsided Development," *The Journal of Economic History*, vol. 21, no. 1 (March 1901): 1-25.

18. On Ismail's ambitious program and its failures, see Robert Tignor, *Modernization and British Rule* (Princeton, N.J.: Princeton University Press, 1966).

19. Gabriel Baer, *Egyptian Guilds in Modern Times*, no. 8 (Jerusalem: The Oriental Society, 1964).

20. "If religion was the cement of the Islamic structure, the corporations were the bricks of which it was built." H.A.R. Gibb and R. Bowen, *Islamic Society and the West*, vol. 1 (Oxford: Oxford University Press, 1950), p. 277.

21. Baer, *Egyptian Guilds*, p. 132.

22. Issawi, "Egypt Since 1800," pp. 4-5.

23. A.E. Crouchley, *The Economic Development of Modern Egypt* (London: Longmans Green, 1938), p. 50.

24. Baer, *Egyptian Guilds*, pp. 130-38.

25. Ibid., p. 133.

26. Ibid., pp. 133-34.

27. Ibid., p. 5.

28. As for the *ulema,* 'Ali was aware of the potential danger it posed to his modernization policies. The Mameluke massacre of 1811 served as a warning to the *ulema.* A British traveler, James Augustus St. John, described the *ulema's* opposition to 'Ali in visiting mosques, bazaars, and schools. See St. John, *Egypt and Mohammed Ali: Travels in the Valley of the Nile,* vol. 1 (London: Longman, 1834), pp. 39-48.

29. Crouchley, *Economic Development,* p. 41.

30. Ibid., p. 67.

31. Baer, *Egyptian Guilds,* pp. 136-37.

32. Ibid., pp. 136-38.

33. Ibid., p. 136. See also Crouchley, *Economic Development,* pp. 72-76.

34. Crouchley, *Economic Development,* p. 72.

35. David Landes, "Japan and Europe, Contrasts in Industrialization," in *The State and Economic Enterprise in Japan,* ed. William W. Lockwood (Princeton, N.J.: Princeton University Press, 1965), pp. 145-53.

36. Ibid., pp. 133-35.

37. David Landes, *Bankers and Pashas* (Cambridge: Harvard University Press), pp. 147-72.

38. Crouchley also maintains that the 1838 commercial treaty between England and the Porte was a blow to 'Ali's state monopoly system. The treaty was designed to break 'Ali's powered profit-making. Crouchley, *Economic Development,* p. 74.

39. Ibid., p. 63.

40. Ibid.

41. Ibid.

42. Halpern, "Middle Eastern Armies," pp. 177-315.

43. Halpern, *The Politics of Social Change,* p. 59.

44. Emil Lederer and Jakob Marschak, "Der Neuer Mittelstand," in *Grundriss der Sozialokonomik,* Sect. 9, 1 (Tubingen, Germany: Tubingen University Press, 1926).

45. Ralf Dahrendorf, *Class and Class Conflict in Industrial Society* (Stanford, Calif.: Stanford University Press, 1959), p. 52.

46. Ibid., pp. 52-53.

47. Ibid., p. 53.

48. Ibid., p. 56.

49. Halpern, *The Politics of Social Change*, p. 274.

50. Ibid., p. 258.

51. Ibid., p. 259.

52. Ibid., p. 258.

53. Ibid.

54. Ibid., pp. 56-57.

55. Ibid., p. 58.

56. Mannheim borrowed this term from Alfred Weber but made wider use of it. See Karl Mannheim, *Ideology and Utopia* (New York: Harcourt Brace, 1952). Mannheim elaborated and modified this concept in his "The Problem of the Intelligentsia," *Essays on the Sociology of Culture* (London: Routledge & Kegan Paul, 1956), pp. 91-170.

57. Halpern, *The Politics of Social Change*, p. 274.

58. Ibid., pp. 76-77.

59. Patrick O'Brien, *The Revolution in Egypt's Economic System* (London: Oxford University Press, 1966).

60. Ibid., pp. 278-80.

61. Harsanyi, "Explanation."

62. O'Brien, *The Revolution in Egypt's Economic System.*

63. Morroe Berger, *Bureaucracy and Society in Modern Egypt* (Princeton, N.J.: Princeton University Press, 1957).

64. See Huntington, *Political Order*, pp. 3-79.

Notes Chapter 4

1. Harold D. Lasswell and Daniel Lerner, eds., *World Revolutionary Elites* (Cambridge, Mass.: M.I.T. Press, 1965), chaps. 1 and 2, pp. 29-96.

2. Dankwart Rustow, "The Study of Elites: Who's Who, When, and How," *World Politics*, 18, no. 4 (July 1966): 690-717.

3. Ibid., p. 701, see also pp. 715-16.

4. Dankwart Rustow, "Political Sociology," *Current History*, 1, no. 3 (1957): 85.

5. See Carl J. Friedrich, *The New Image of the Common Man*,

2nd ed. (Boston: Little Brown and Co., 1950), pp. 257-58, 370, fn. 12; and Meisel's critique of Friedrich's interpretation of the Mosca-Pareto elite concept in James H. Meisel, *The Myth of the Ruling Class: Gaetano Mosca and the Elite* (Ann Arbor: University of Michigan, 1962), pp. 356-60. See also T.B. Bottomore, *Elites and Society* (New York: Basic Books, 1964), pp. 1-15.

6. Rustow, "The Study of Elites," p. 711.

7. I have borrowed some of Professor Keller's criteria for the ruling class, without accepting Keller's universality of elite types—the strategic elites, or strategic types.

8. The difference between a bureaucratic class and a ruling class is that the latter is made up of the political leadership who rise to power by exercising their political ability. See Bottomore, *Elites and Society,* n. 78.

9. Ibid., pp. 86-104.

10. Rustow, "The Study," pp. 715-16, feels that elite theorists from Marx to Michels "formulated comprehensive statements about ruling classes . . . sustained by inadequate evidence. . . ."

11. Ralf Dahrendorf, *Class and Class Conflict in Industrial Society* (Stanford, California: Stanford University Press, 1959).

12. Ibid.

13. Robert Dahl, "The Concept of Power," *Behavioral Science,* 2, no. 2 (July 1967): 201-18; "A Critique of the Ruling Elite Model," *American Political Science Review,* 52:2 (June, 1958): 463-69; *Who Governs?* (New Haven, Connecticut: Yale University Press, 1961), pp. 1-12, 271-325. See also Daniel Bell, *The End of Ideology,* rev. ed., (New York: Collier Books, 1966), pp. 47-74; and Talcott Parsons, *Structure and Process in Modern Societies* (Glencoe, Ill.: Free Press, 1960), pp. 199-225.

14. Dahl, "A Critique of the Ruling Elite Model."

15. Ibid.

16. James Heaphey, "Organization of Egypt: Inadequacies of a Non-Political Model for Nation-Building" *World Politics,* vol. 18, no. 2 (January 1966): 186-88.

17. See Eliezer Be'eri, *The Officer Class in Arab Politics and Society,* (New York: Praeger, 1970).

18. The following statistics are taken from Eliezer Be'eri, *Ha-ktsuna Ve'hashilton B'Olam Ha'aravi* (Hebrew) (Merhavia, Israel: Sifriat Poalim, 1966).

19. With the exception of the UAR government, 1958-1961.

20. Be'eri, *The Officer Class*, pp. 287-93.

21. Ibid., pp. 293-350.

22. Ibid., pp. 24-40.

23. Suzanne Keller, *Beyond the Ruling Class: Strategic Elites in Modern Society* (New York: Random House, 1963), p. 32.

24. Ibid.

25. Ibid., p. 290.

26. Be'eri, "Social Origin."

27. We are grateful here to ideas provided by Reinhardt Bendix and Seymour Martin Lipset's "Political Sociology," in *Current Sociology,* 6, no. 2 (1957): 83-87.

28. Ibid., p. 84.

29. Gabriel Baer, *History of Landownership* (New York: Oxford University Press, 1962), pp. 177-78.

30. Patrick O'Brien, "An Economic Appraisal of the Egyptian Revolution," *The Journal of Development Studies,* 1, no. 1 (October 1964): 99.

31. Leonard Binder, "Crisis in Political Mobilization," in *Political Parties and Political Development,* ed. Joseph La Palombara and Myron Weiner (Princeton, N.J.: Princeton University Press, 1966), p. 235.

32. Ibid., Table 3, Category 5, pp. 237-38.

33. Ibid., p. 237; Be'eri, *The Officer Class,* pp. 297-98.

34. Keller, *Beyond the Ruling Class,* p. 32.

35. O'Brien, "An Economic Appraisal."

36. Charles Issawi, *Egypt in Revolution: An Economic Analysis* (New York: Oxford University Press, 1965), Table 12, p. 120.

37. Binder, "Crisis in Political Mobilization," Table 3, p. 237.

38. Binder argues that this was an improvement over the old regime. For now, labor has political access to the official establishment of the government. Through their legitimation as government employees, workers can secure redress which they could not obtain in the past; Ibid., p. 232.

39. Ibid., Table 3, Category 6, p. 237.

40. Ibid.

41. Baer, *History of Landownership.*

42. The 1965 volume of *Ruz al-Yusuf* describes feudal corruption in villages and states that some *'umdahs,* through legal procedures, can deprive peasants of their land. They do this through their administrative powers as governmental representatives and, in some cases, as directors of cooperatives. *Al-Ahram* and *al-Gumhuriyyah* issues of May 1966 give full descriptions of the trials and errors of land reform in Egypt, and "the struggle against feudalism."

43. O'Brien, "An Economic Appraisal," p. 99.

44. Uriel Dann, *Iraq Under Qassem* (Jerusalem: Israel Universities Press, 1969), pp. 19-32.

45. On the crisis of political participation in Egypt see Leonard Binder, "Political Recruitment," in La Palombara and Weiner, *Political Parties,* pp. 217-40.

46. Huntington, "Political Development," p. 419.

47. For a similar argument on the Maghreb based on attitudinal and psychological insights, see Douglas E. Ashford, *Elite Value and Attitudinal Change in the Maghreb* (Bloomington, Indiana: Indiana University Press, 1966).

48. Huntington, "Political Development."

Notes Chapter 5

1. Samuel P. Huntington, *Political Order in Changing Societies* (New Haven: Yale University Press, 1968), Chap. 5. Amos Perlmutter, *Political Institutionalization* (Cambridge: Center for International Affairs, Harvard University, no. 25, 1968).

2. Majid Khadduri, *Independent Iraq* (London, Oxford University Press, 1968). Amos Perlmutter, "From Obscurity to Rule: The Syrian Army and the Ba'th party" *Western Political Quarterly* vol. 22, no. 4 (December 1969).

3. *President Gamal Abdul Nasser's Speeches and Press Interviews,* January-December 1961, published by the Egyptian government, 1961, p. 395.

4. Ibid., p. 396.

5. Eliezer Be'eri, *The Officer Class in Arab Politics and Society,* Praeger (New York, 1970), and Jean Lacouture and Simmone Lacouture, *Egypt in Transition* (New York: Criterion Books, 1958).

6. Be'eri, *The Officer Class,* p. 75.

7. Jean and Simmone Lacouture, *Egypt in Transition,* pp. 141-45; Be'eri, *The Officer Class,* pp.

8. Ihsan Abdal-Qudus in *Al-akhbar,* 1954.

9. Richard P. Mitchell, *The Society of the Muslim Brothers* (London: Oxford University Press, 1969); Be'eri, *The Officer Class;* Lacouture and Lacouture, *Egypt in Transition.*

10. Shimon Shamir, "Five Years of the Organization of Liberation Rally in Egypt," *The New East* vol. 8, no. 32 (1951), p. 263.

11. Ibid., p. 264.

12. Ibid., p. 278.

13. Be'eri, *The Officer Class,* pp.

14. Ibid.

15. *Al-Ahram,* June 24, 1956.

16. Article 192 of the new Egyptian Constitution as published in *Al-Ahram,* January 1, 1956. Author's translation. The clause may also be found in the *U.A.R. Yearbook,* 1960 (Cairo: Information Department, 1960).

17. Anwar al-Sadat, *Qa'idah Sha'biyyah (People's Base)* Cairo: June 1958), quoted in *Middle East Review* (1960): 478.

18. Ibid., p. 37.

19. Curtis Jones, "The New Egyptian Constitution," *The Middle East Journal* 8, no. 4 (Summer 1956): 300.

20. *Egyptian Gazette,* July 29, September 4, and December 12, 1960, quoted in Itzchak Oron, ed., *Middle East Record, 1960* (hereafter cited as MER) I (London: Weidenfeld and Nicolson, 1962), pp. 467-68.

21. See, for example, the speech delivered in Damascus, February 24, 1961, in Nasser, *Speeches and Press Interviews,* pp. 53-57.

22. Ibid.

23. Ibid., p. 51.

24. *Egyptian Gazette,* December 12, 1960.

25. *MER,* p. 479.

26. *Al-Ahram,* June 12, 1960, pp. 2-3.

27. *U.A.R. Yearbook,* 1960, pp. 31-32.

28. *Al-Ahram,* May-June 1960.

29. Colonel 'Abd al-Hamid Sarraj, a pro-Nasser Ba'thist, was appointed Secretary General, relieving Anwar al-Sadat, in 1960.

30. The Majlis was dissolved despite Syrian opposition. See *Al-Hayat,* January 5, 1960; also *al-Ayyam,* January 30, 1960.

31. Full text in *al-Ahram,* March 27, 1960, pp. 3-4.

32. MER 1960, p. 491; *U.A.R. Yearbook,* 1960, pp. 31-32.

33. Nasser, *Speeches and Press Interviews,* p. 83; al-Sadat, *Qa'idah,* pp. 22-27.

34. *Economist* (March 12, 1960), pp. 974-77.

35. This began as early as spring 1959, during a general convention of Ba'th delegates from all the Arab states. In September 1959, the Ba'th leader and UAR Northern Region Minister for Culture and National Guidance, Riyad al-Maliki, resigned. The Ba'th itself split; in mid-1960, 'Abdallah al-Rimawi, the party's Secretary General in Jordan, established a rival National Command in Damascus, denounced the Syrian Ba'th, and hailed the UAR as champion of all Arabs. In December 1960, Akram al-Hawrani, then Minister of Justice, in the UAR central government, resigned. Mass resignation of Ba'th ministers, at both levels of the UAR, followed. *Middle East Record* (1960): 497-507.

36. Since we are dealing here mainly with the National Union, the UAR merger is discussed only in passing. For a recent interpretation of the union, its merger, and collapse see Patrick Seale, *The Struggle for Syria* (London: Oxford University Press, 1968), pp. 307-26; Malcolm Kerr, *The Arab Cold War 1958-1967,* 2nd ed., (London: Oxford University Press, 1967), pp. 97-137; Kemel Saleh Abu Jabar, "The Arab Ba'th Socialist Party; History, Ideology and Organization," Ph. D. diss., Syracuse University, 1965, pp. 106-50.

37. The new program was directed by Nasser's trusted Minister for Presidential Affairs, 'Ali Sabri.

38. Sarah Lulko, "The Popular Organization of the Nasserite Regime," mimeographed, Tel-Aviv, 1970, p. 5.

39. I am most grateful to Sarah Lulko of the Shiloah Institute of Tel-Aviv for suggesting this to me.

40. Ibid., p. 7.

41. 'Ali Sabri, "State Ensured," *Egyptian Gazette,* p. 6.

42. Ibid.

43. The entire July 1961 issue of *Egyptian Economic and Political Review* (EEPR) is devoted to the *Economic Development Organization* (EDO). For a summary of economic activities, see

Malcolm Kerr, "The Emergence of a Socialist Ideology in Egypt," *The Middle East Journal*, 16, no. 2 (1962): 127-44. For the best concise evaluation of the Egyptian economy since Nasser see Patrick K. O'Brien, "An Economic Appraisal of the Egyptian Revolution," *The Journal of Development Studies*, 1, no. 1 (October 1964): 93-113, and his *The Revolution in Egypt's Economic System* (London: Oxford University Press, 1966).

44. Lulko, "The Popular Organization," p. 8.

45. *Al-Ahram*, July 3, 1964, pp. 2-3.

46. Leonard Binder, "Political Recruitment and Participation in Egypt," in Joseph La Palombara and Myron Weiner, *Political Parties and Political Development* (Princeton, N.J.: Princeton University Press, 1966), p. 234.

47. I am grateful to Sarah Lulko for this invaluable information. See Lulko, "The Popular Organization," pp. 8-13.

48. On the lack of balance between political policy making institutions and bureaucratic policy implementing structures, and the conflict between military officers and civilian officers see Fred Riggs, "Bureaucracy and Political Development" in La Polembara *Political Parties* (Princeton, N.J.: Princeton University Press, 1963), pp. 120-67; also S.N. Eisenstadt, "Bureaucracy and Political Development," ibid., pp. 107-08.

Notes Chapter 6

1. Lulko, "The Popular Organization." Some of the information is based on synopsis of *MER, 1967* ed. Daniel Dishon (Jerusalem: Israel Universities Press, 1971). See the sections on the UAR written by S. Lulko and S. Shamir, pp. 529-50. An excellent reference work is Menahem Mansoor, *Political and Diplomatic History of the Arab World 1900-1967*, vol. 5, 1965-1967, (Washington, D.C.: Microcard editions). See the months of April, May and June, 1967.

2. Ibid., p. 563.

3. Sarah Lulko, "The Popular Organization of the Nasserite Regime," (Tel-Aviv, mimeographed, 1970), p. 5.

4. *Al Taliah*, 1968.

5. Ibid., p. 7.

6. Ibid.

7. Only some reliable information is available on Army-ASU relations. See n. 13 below.

8. See Chapter 2.

9. Ibid.

10. Robert Stephens, *Nasser* (New York: Simon and Schuster, 1971), p. 359.

11. Haykal, *al-Ahram* (Cairo) May 24, 1967.

12 Ibid.

13. Information on Army-Nasser struggle found in Stephens, *Nasser*, pp. 358-63 and Anthony Nutting, *Nasser* (New York: E.P. Dutton, 1972), pp. 338-57.

14. Most of the information on the coup is collected from the Arab and Israeli presses. Until the trials of the anti-Sadat group began, we were in possession only of Egyptian and pro-Egyptian Lebanese newspaper information. However bizarre, gossipy and exaggerated the claims are for the Sadat group (we know the story told only by the latter), I find the accounts of the basic personality conflicts, uses of established political bases of power, chicanery, spying, tapping and so on, not unusual or untrue. Basically the stories do not deviate from Nasserist or historical Egyptian practices.

15. General Sa'd Shazli, the new (as of May 1971) Chief of Staff was a company commander in the 1948 war and surrendered with the Egyptian army in Faluja in 1949. In the 1956 war he was a paratroop battalion commander and retreated with the defeated army. In 1967 as the general commanding the key southwestern Sinai front, his army was annihilated by Israeli General Arik Sharon. In Yemen he was not distinguished and his section of the southern Suez during the war of attrition was infiltrated several times by the Israelis. In 1973, General Shazli commanded the successful Egyptian crossing of the Suez Canal into Sinai. However, as soon as General Sharon crossed to the western bank of the canal, bled the Second Army and encircled the Third Army, General Shazli, like other Egyptian generals, moved to a defensive position. If not for the U.S.-engineered ceasefire, Shazli's armies would have surrendered or been annihilated. Generals Mourtageh (the Chief of Staff on the Egyptian expedition to Yemen), Riad and Sadiq are also veterans of the 1967 and the Yemen defeats. General Fawzi shared defeat with the Jordanian army when he commanded the "united" Egyptian-Jordanian armies in 1967.

16. On the Sadat-Sabri struggle over the projected new UAR union, see *Al-Ahram*, May 14, 1971, May 16, 1971, and *Maariv*, May 16, 1971 and May 18, 1971.

17. Sadat's domestic chief now is Major Abdal al-Qadar Hatem, a veteran Free Officer and Nasser's first propaganda minister (1953-55) ousted by Nasser for personal ambition. Several other disgruntled Nasserists, civilian and military, have been reinstated by Sadat. Most prominent is the hidden power of the Muhi-al-Din brothers. Hatem is now Egypt's prime minister.

INDEX

228

Hunter, Floyd, 110
Huntington, Samuel P.: on harnessing
  political mobilization, 128-29
on military praetorianism, 11
on military professionalism, 9n, 57
on political institutionalization, 11, 12,
  128
Husain, Kamal al-Din, 46, 49, 50, 68-69,
  149
Husain, Taha, *The Future of Culture in
  Egypt,* 34
Hussein, King, 57, 184

Ibrahim, Hasan, 50, 139, 143
Ikhtarna Lak (We Have Chosen for You)
  series, 59-61, 76, 105
Imperialism (*Al-Isti'mar*), 145-46
India, 12, 39-40
Indonesia, 17, 18, 128
Industry, Egyptian: decline of, during
  Muhammad 'Ali's regime, 86-89, 90
  effect of British occupation on, 89-90
Intelligentsia, 101-102, 103, 105
Iqbal, Mahomed, 64
Iraq, 15, 19
  civilian intervention in the military of,
    13-14
  introduction of arbitrator regime type
    in, 134
  1958 Qassem coup in, 127
Islam, 39-40, 43-45
  Muslim Brotherhood on, 42
  problem of relation of Arabism to,
    61-66
Islamic Call, The (Muhammad Mustafa
  'Ata), 60, 75-76
Isma'il, Khedive, 25-26, 33, 55, 86
Israel: Egypt's Six Days War with, 126,
  176-81, 184, 201
  war of October 1973, 203
Israel Defense Forces (IDF), 177
Issawi, Charles, 123

Jadid, Salah, 195
Janissaries, 53, 54
Japan, bureaucracy of, compared with
  Egypt, 91
Jews, attitudes of Muslim Brotherhood
  and Nasserites toward, compared, 67

See also Israel
Jinnah, Muhammad, 39
Johnson, John J., on role of military in
  New Middle Class, 82-83, 84, 95, 97
Jordan: army of, 56-57
  end of Nasserite domination over, 184
Justice Party (Turkey), 13

Kamal, Mustafa Khalil, 143
Kamil, Mustafa, 31-32, 34, 36, 79, 199
Keller, Suzanne, 122
Kemalist legacy in Turkey, 8, 131
Kerr, Malcolm H., 64
Kinship system, 30

Lacourture, Jean and Simmone, *Egypt in
  Transition,* 1
Landes, David, 91
Landownership, 118-121
  class, growth of, in Egypt, 92
Laski, Harold, 60
Lasswell, Harold D., 108
Latif al-Baghdadi, *see* 'Abd al-Latif al-
  Baghdadi
Latin America, 8
Law of Local Government (*Qanun
  Nizam al-Idarah al-Mahalliyyah*), 151
Leadership, attitudes of Muslim Brother-
  hood and Nasserites toward, compared,
  77-78
Lederer, Emil, 97, 99
Lenin, V.I., 66, 155, 172
Liberal nationalists, 33-37
Liberation Institute, 59
Liberation Rally (Hai'at al-Tahrir),
  156-157
  formation of, 47-48, 49-52
  political functions of, 163
  structure of, 140-41
  See also Revolutionary Command
    Council
Libya-Egypt union, 193, 196
Lipset, S.M., 108

Majid, Abdul, 54
Mamelukes, 21, 22, 24
Mannheim, Karl, 101-102
Mao Tse-tung, 155, 161
Mar'i, Sayyid, 143
Marschak, Jakob, 97, 99

Marx, Karl, 95, 98
Michels, Roberto, 108, 109, 110
Middle Class, New (NMC): army as most cohesive stratum of, 100-105
Egypt's failure to develop entrepreneurial, 86-93
relationship between Egyptian army and, 81-86
theories of, 93-100
Middle class, rural: benefits of Egyptian social revolution for, 118-22
relationship between army and, 124-25
Military, Egyptian: British reduction of, 27
characteristics of, leading to its praetorian role, 57-59
control of, by Society of Free Officers, 49-50
dependence of Sadat regime on, 200-201
impact on praetorianism of frequent civilian intervention in, 13-14, 42-43
as most cohesive stratum of New Middle Class, 81-85, 100-105
Muhammad 'Ali's reform of, 23-24, 55-56
and political mobilization, 105-6
power struggle between ASU and, 185-88
purge of, 181-84
relationship between rural middle class and, 124-25
role of, in a praetorian state, 4-8
Soviet aid to, 201-3
and 'Urabi Officer Movement, 26-27
See also Praetorianism
Military professionalism: defined, 9 and n
relation of, to praetorianism, 14-15
Mills, C. Wright, 110-11
Ministry of Agrarian Reform, 143
Ministry of Communications, 143
Ministry of Industry, 143
Misr al-Fatat (Young Egypt), 14, 42-43, 46
Misr Wa-Risaltuha (Egypt's Mission), 69-70
Mitchell, Richard P., 44
Modernization, Egyptian: conflict between center and periphery in movements of, 28-29, 30

conflict between tradition and, 63-65
Great Britain's contributions to, 29-30
Muhammad 'Ali's program of, 21-25, 26, 30

Moltke, Helmuth von, 54
Mosca, Gaetano, 108, 109, 110
Muhammad 'Ali, 3, 31
decline of Egyptian industry during reign of, 86-90
growth in landowning class under, 91-92
legacy of, 185, 187
modernization program implemented by, 21-25, 26
his reforms of the army, 23-24, 55-56
reign of, characterized as patrimonial, 27-28

Muhi al-Din, Khalid, 50, 139, 187
Muhi al-Din, Zakariyya, 162, 179, 187
and anti-Sadat coup, 189
and Free Officer Corps, 139
and Nasser's resignation, 183
and Revolutionary Command Council, 49, 182

Mun'in 'Abd al-Ra'uf, 'Abd al-, *see* 'Abd al-Mun'im 'Abd al-Ra'uf
Mu'nis, Husain, *Misr Wa-Risaltuha* (Egypt's Mission), 69-70

Muslim Brotherhood, 38-39, 104, 140, 141, 156
attitude of, toward Egypt, 67-71
attitude of, toward Islam, economic reform and society, 74-77
attitude of, toward leadership, 77-78
attitude of, toward patriotism and nationalism, 71-74
attitude of, toward political parties and organizations, 78-80
attitude of, toward West and modernization, 66-67
ideology of, 41-42
infiltration of the army by, 43
recruitment of urban middle classes by, 36-37
relations with army of, 14, 18
relations with Free Officers of, 46-47, 48, 49
relations with Liberation Rally of, 50-51
success and popularity of, 44, 45

and restriction of political participation, 128

Political mobilization: and the military, 105-6

restriction of, by Nasser's ruling elite, 127, 128-29

Political parties: attitudes of Muslim Brotherhood and Nasserites toward, 78-80

collapse of, 40-41, 48, 50

effect on praetorianism of weak and ineffective, 12-13

formation of Egyptian, 31-33

stabilization and institutionalization of, necessary for nonpraetorian system, 130

Popular Socialist Party (*al-Hizb al-jumhuriyyah al-Ishtarakiyyah*), 156

Praetorian armies, *see* Arbitrator type of praetorian army; Ruler type of praetorian army

Praetorianism: contrasted with patrimonialism, 52-54

correlates of, 7

discussion of, 4-8

entrenchment of, in Egypt, 200-203

political conditions contributing to, 11-15, 47, 107

variables leading to, 10-11

See also Arbitrator type of praetorian army; Military; Ruler type of praetorian army

Preparatory Committee (1961), 122, 124, 159

Propaganda, *see Ikhtarna Lak* series

Public Sector, of Egyptian economy, 171

Pye, Lucian, 82, 83

Qaddafi, Mu'amer, 196, 197

Qa'idah Sha'biyyah (The Popular Base), 144, 148-49

Qasim, 'Abd al-Karim, 17

Qudus, Ikhsan 'Abd al-, 156, 157, 192

Quwwatli, Shukri al-, 148

Raid, Mahmud, 189, 191

Ra'uf, 'Abd al-Mun'im 'Abd al-, *see* 'Abd al-Mun'im 'Abd al-Ra'uf

Raziq, 'Ali 'Abd al-, 34

Religion, authority of, on local level, 30, 31

Revolutionary Command Council (RCC), 132, 133, 135, 137

abolishment of, 112

and Arab Socialist Union, 156-57

origin and function of, 48-51, 138, 140-42

Sadat on, 144

See also Liberation Rally

Riad, Mahmud, 116, 189, 194

Rifa't, Kamal, 147

Rivlin, Helen, 22

Rogers, William, 194

Royal Institute of International Affairs, 48-49

Ruler type of praetorian army, 6, 8-11, 15

attitudes and behavior of, 10

basic characteristics of, 16-17

compared with arbitrator type, 131-34

development of political ideology by, 17-20

evolution of, 135-37

subtypes of, 17

See also Arbitrator type of praetorian army

Russell, Bertrand, 60

Rustow, Dankwart, 108

Ruz al-Yusuf, 151, 156

Sabbagh, Salah al-Din al-, 19

Sabri, 'Ali, 187

and anti-Sadat coup, 188-194 passim

and Arab Socialist Union (pre-1967), 158, 160-66

and Arab Socialist Union (post-1967), 167-71

viewed as possible successor to Nasser, 186

Sadat, Anwar al-, 46, 50, 182, 187

abortive coup against (May 1971), 167, 184, 188-95

appointed Secretary General of Islamic Congress, 143-44

compared with Nasser, 196, 198, 203

dependence of regime of, on the military, 3, 112

-Faisal entente, 196-97

and Free Officers, 50, 139

on National Union, 144

restrictiveness of his regime, 110, 114
and Revolutionary Command Council,
49
and Soviet aid, 202-3
strategic elites under, 115-16
support of military for, 185, 200-1
viewed as interim president, 186
and war with Israel, 176-77
Sadiq, Muhammad, 201, 202
and anti-Sadat coup, 189, 190, 191,
193
Sadiq, Yusuf, 49
Safran, Nadav, 27
Sa'id, Pasha, 89
Salem, Gamal, 139, 143, 187
Salem, Salah, 139, 187
Saud, King, 73
Sawt-al-Arab (Cairo Broadcasting and
TV system), 192
Sayyid, Lutfi al-, 32, 34, 36
al-Jaridah, 35
Shafi'i, Husain al-, 46, 49, 189
Sharaf, Sami, 186, 187
and anti-Sadat coup, 188-89, 190, 192,
193, 194
Shauqi, Ahmad, 50
Shazli, Muhammad Sa'd, 189, 190, 191,
193, 201
Shils, Edward, 82, 83
Shishakly, Adib, 19, 127, 137
Shuqair, Labib, 189
Sidqi, 'Aziz, 143
Six Days War (1967), 126, 176-81, 184,
201
Socialism, Egyptian and Arab, 146-48
Socialist Union, *see* Arab Socialist Union
Socialist Youth organization, 171
Society, attitudes of Muslim Brother-
hood and Nasserites toward, compared,
74-77
Society of Free Officers, *see under* Free
Officer Corp.
Soviet Union, 178, 179, 180, 193-94
support of Egypt by, 201-3
Stalin, Joseph, 178
Strachey, John, 60
Suez Canal, 159
Sukarno, Achmed, 18, 104
Sulaiman, Sidqui, 162
Suleiman the Magnificent, 54
Sultanism, 53

Syria, 104, 203
ALM in, 135
army of, 8, 14
attempted union with Egypt, 144-45,
146, 148-56
coups in, 127
establishment of military dictatorship
in, 19
introduction of arbitrator regime type
in, 134
introduction of ruler regime type in,
137
Tal'at, Hasan, 189
Tali'ah, al- (magazine), 171-72, 173,
188, 190, 192
Trade unions, support for Nasser from,
124
Triple Revolution, 145-47
Turkey: civilian intervention in military
affairs of, 13
Kemalist legacy in, 8, 131

'Ukasha, Tawrat, 139
Ummah party, 32
UNEF (United Nations Emergency
Forces), 179
United Arab Republic: debate over
drafting of permanent constitution for,
168-70
end of, 156
formation of, 145-56
United States, 203
ceasefire imposed on Israel by, 184
Egyptian rapprochement with, 179,
194
University Students' Union, 140
'Urabi Officer Movement (1879-1882),
26-27, 57, 58
Urban workers, skilled, benefits of
Egyptian social revolution for, 122-29

Vatikiotis, P.J., 49

Wafd party, 18, 48, 140
failure of, 41-42
organization of, 31
popularity of, 32, 58-59
taken over by landowners, 12, 32-33,
36, 37, 40

233